T0305821

ORGANIZING AROUND INTELLIGENCE

ORGANIZING AROUND INTELLIGENCE

Liang Thow Yick

World Scientific

NEW JERSEY · LONDON · SINGAPORE · SHANGHAI · HONG KONG · TAIPEI · CHENNAI

Published by

World Scientific Publishing Co. Pte. Ltd.

5 Toh Tuck Link, Singapore 596224

USA office: 27 Warren Street, Suite 401-402, Hackensack, NJ 07601

UK office: 57 Shelton Street, Covent Garden, London WC2H 9HE

British Library Cataloguing-in-Publication Data
A catalogue record for this book is available from the British Library.

First published 2004
Reprinted 2006

ORGANIZING AROUND INTELLIGENCE

ISBN-13 978-981-238-731-8
ISBN-10 981-238-731-5

Typeset by Stallion Press
E-mail: enquiries@stallionpress.com

Printed in Singapore

Dedicated to

Char Hoon

Zhen Ning, Justin

Wei Ning, Nicole

Preface

At the dawn of the new millennium, an understanding and exploitation of scientific concepts and opportunities represent a fresh niche in economic activities. An emerging breed of entrepreneurs, the technopreneurs, forms the vital driving force behind many highly developed economies. The new explorers are inspired by scientific innovations that can provide them with a quantum leap in their business endeavors. The competitive edge they seek is the techno-advantage. Examples of such emerging opportunities are embedded in domains such as the life sciences and the e-landscape.

On a broader perspective, in leadership, management philosophy and strategy, and social dynamics, comprehending a new scientific domain that integrates complexity, evolution, nonlinearity and intelligence is crucial for all human organizations (businesses, government bodies, institutions of learning, communities/societies, economies and nations). Humankind is beginning to realize that the universe and its microcosms are more a mind than a machine. In addition, these systems are complex, nonlinear and adaptive. Inevitably, the human mind and the vicissitudes of life are nonlinear in nature. For simplicity and comfort, the nonlinear dimension has all along been suppressed or ignored. In actuality, lots of opportunities are embedded in nonlinear spaces and at the edge of chaos. It is in these spaces where innovation and creativity are skilfully camouflaged, awaiting the arrival of appropriate intelligent decoders.

The exploitation of complexity and evolution theories is spreading across some advanced economies. However, the holistic application of this domain in human organizations requires a paradigmatic shift in thinking and a much more in-depth reflection. Thus, the changes in environment and understanding warrant a fresh mindset and a totally re-defined approach towards leading, structuring and managing human organizations. The primary focus of the new mindset is the human mind. The mental state and knowledge structures of the human thinking system are of primary significance. The new strategy is to organize around intelligence (intelligence strategy). Such an endeavor requires a lot of patience and time.

The human mind is an example of an entity known as complex adaptive system. The human mind—indeed, a business corporation, a society, the whole of nature, and the entire universe—is steered by intelligence. Intrinsic intelligence, a unique form of energy, is responsible for the formation of structure, processing of information, structuring of knowledge, as well as comprehension of evolution phenomena. Intelligence is the energy that drives the universe and it is also the entity that nature has created to unlock itself.

A simple biological organism that learns, evolves and adapts to the environment is a localized order that has been initiated and created by intelligence. Intelligence when manifested up to a certain level of development exhibits nonlinear characteristics and supports the emergence of life and consciousness. Life cannot exist without the presence of intelligence. On the same basis, for a human organization to survive and compete in a knowledge-intensive environment, it must possess its own orgmind, consciousness and collective intelligence. Thus, the three attributes, life, intelligence and structure, are inseparable.

Apparently, intelligence is the mysterious energy that orchestrates and drives the entire dynamic of the universe, and the evolution of all forms of structures and lives in this world. This is the fundamental principle of the intelligent organization theory to be discussed in this book. The theory stipulates that any artificial group created by humankind, from a business organization to a nation, must also focus on intelligence and collective intelligence, if the system is to evolve successfully. In such an artifact, intelligence-related entities and activities form the germination centers for structure to be erected. Spontaneously, order and the physical structure will emerge from the deep nonlinear dynamics/processes.

Fundamentally, the core of the intelligent organization theory emphasizes the development of a mindset that focuses on intelligence as the impetus behind mindfulness, awareness, connectivity, learning, thinking, knowledge internalization, decision-making and adaptation (the intelligence paradigm). The keys to optimize benefits from the global intelligence revolution are better awareness and mindfulness that embrace the ability to utilize the human thinking systems better, and the skill to quickly establish useful relationships/connectivity that can nurture a more supportive/mindful culture. Mindfulness and awareness are the primary mental functions that are created by human consciousness. Thus, in a more competitive and fast-paced environment, the nonlinear aspect of intelligence and the associated properties of complexity such as the butterfly effect and rugged landscape must be more thoroughly comprehended and appropriately utilized.

Consequently, a new mode of leadership and management must be cultivated. It is important to recognize that organizing around intelligence is the primary phenomenon that nature adopts to create and sustain order, structure and life in the midst of complexity.

The autopoietic and self-organizing dynamics manifested in such complex adaptive systems defy the expanding universe concept of increasing entropy and disorder. The evolutionary processes, if intelligent enough, will creatively manipulate and extract new information from the edge of chaos to further strengthen existing order. In particular, by channelling intense intelligence into the edge of chaos, and through the proper exploitation of its nonlinear characteristic, a small investment could result in a large return (the butterfly effect). This is a basic aspect of the intelligence strategy that a smart evolver must adopt. The advantage to be exploited is the intelligence advantage. In this respect, this book will be beneficial to leaders and managers/executives of businesses, government bodies, institutions of learning, communities and nations. It will also be a useful reference source for researchers in numerous other organization-related domains.

Finally, it must be emphasized that the mindset and the concepts to be presented and discussed in this book engulf a current research frontier that cuts across numerous disciplines. The intelligent organization theory is an integrated theory that human organizations must adopt to emerge as victors in the intelligence revolution. However, new ideas in this domain are still unfolding dramatically everyday. The primary objective of this book is merely to create a fresh awareness and to point a new direction. Therefore, the readers (in particular, leaders and potential leaders of all human organizations) must explore this work with a flexible and open mind. As some of the concepts are rather abstract, they are built up gradually (with some repetitions) over the chapters.

For those who are enchanted by this new knowledge domain and would like to catch more glimpses of it, may I wish you happy reading!

Liang Thow Yick

Contents

I am convinced that the nations and people who master the new sciences of complexity will become the economic, cultural, and political superpowers of the next century.

Heinz Pagels, The Dreams of Reason

I
Entering the Intelligence Era

This chapter introduces the changes taking place in the world that are affecting human organizations as well as all individuals. In particular, the relevant properties of chaos and complexity theory are examined. The fact that the edge of chaos is an unexplored space embedded with new opportunities is highlighted. The observation indicates that a change in era is inevitable.

1.1. Introduction

Over the last two decades, the entire world economy has been drifting from a machine-based setup to an information-based environment. More recently, certain highly developed economies/nations are in fact directing their attention and resources towards establishing a knowledge-based structure. As the reward for high-value-added knowledge and information-intensive activities is much greater, inevitably in the new millennium, all of humankind is gravitating towards the nucleus of the information era, the intelligence era.

The rampant changes sweeping across the world cannot be dealt with simply by means of superficial cosmetic surgery. The unprecedented impact experienced requires more than just some ad hoc structural alterations. To accommodate the formidable developments, a transformation in mindset is necessary. For all human organizations (businesses, communities, economies, nations), the most fundamental transformation points towards organizing around intrinsic intelligence rather than around machines or functions. Complexity, evolution, and intelligence, and the human thinking systems are new areas that need to be scrutinized.

A shift in mindset is an extremely significant event in human history. Such a transformation marks the end of an existing belief and the beginning of a new understanding. It is tantamount to a change in era. The change from a machine mindset to an intelligence mindset indicates that human civilization is entering a new level of consciousness. The higher level of consciousness, if accomplished, will render certain obscurities explicit. The new understanding will identify new territories for exploration and will lead to fresh opportunities/niches. Eventually, the deeper comprehension of evolution and co-evolution of complex adaptive systems and its composite complex adaptive system will lead to the establishment of a higher order of existence.

1.2. Some Major World Changes

In this respect, it is imperative to identify and examine more rigorously the major developments that initiate the above transformation. Some of the crucial events that have exerted unprecedented pressure on human civilization are as follows (illustrated in Fig. 1.1):

a. All of human civilization has drifted rather deeply into the information era but many of the socio-economic systems, structured like machines that support the requirements of the industrial era, are still intact. Thus, there exists a glaring mismatch between new visions and the present structure of human organizations. And accomplishing these new visions is difficult, if

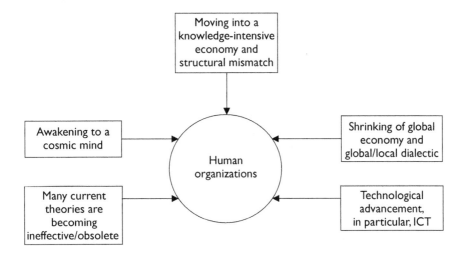

Fig. 1.1. Some major changes affecting humankind and its organizations.

not impossible. Consequently, compared to biological systems, existing human organizations appear to be semi-paralyzed.

b. In addition, a global economy has been emerging and competition is no longer confined locally. The global/local dialectic is a new challenge that both individual and organization are experiencing. Being able to adjust to the new perspective is crucial. The rapid pace of the global environmental changes is an added area of concern. Comprehending and reacting swiftly to environmental changes has become a universal critical success factor. (Speed is also associated with the ability to recognize the shortest path.) Being able to be environmentally proactive, that is, being able to influence the environment, is a new advantage. Today, most human organizations are still not intelligent enough to act and react in the desired manner.

c. Next, the rapid advancement of technological developments, in particular, information and communications technology (ICT), has substantially increased the potential of better connectivity. Quality connectivity is a significant property of intelligent systems. Understanding connectivity and establishing well-connected networks spreading across geographical boundaries are new challenges. The present focus on connectivity is very much restricted to the level of the physical structure. Many organizations are still ignorant as to how the connectivity of the deep structure can be better established and how virtual team can be nurtured. They are not fully aware of its implications and significance.

d. Besides, the current economic theories of equilibrium, perfect rationality and decreasing returns are incapable of explaining the highly dynamic global economy. The existing organization and decision theories that concentrate on linear models, such as game theories and business process re-engineering, are also revealing in their inadequacy. In general, the expansion and domination of the standard reductionist analytic approach of Newtonian deterministic science is manifesting its limits. Therefore, new scientific concepts in the Einsteinian domain must be used to explore and optimize the socio-economic phenomena. Beyond physics, the quantum domain is still a new and unexplored knowledge area.

e. The fifth and extremely important factor is the awakening to a cosmic mind and its nonlinear dynamics. The humankind is beginning to realize and understand that the universe is more a mind than a machine. The human world together with its entire socio-economic and political systems and subsystems, congruous with the natural biological and physical systems, has both linear and nonlinear components. They are complex adaptive systems in which order and disorder co-exist. Such systems consume new information and learn to adapt continuously. It appears that the entire cosmic world and its microcosm, including human organizations, are driven by intelligence.

1.3. Chaos and Complexity Theory

The last factor mentioned above arises from the science of chaos. This new scientific theory was first recognized and investigated by Edward Lorenz, Stephen Smale, and several others in the 1960s. Consciousness, complexity connectivity, dissipation and emergence were identified as the five core properties of this universe and its microcosms (see Fig. 1.2).

A decade later, the focus was shifted to complexity theory, which dealt with the deterministic aspect of chaos (Stuart Kauffman, Christopher Langton and others). The central axiom of the theory is the inseparability of order and complexity, that is, the universe is inherently chaotic and intrinsically orderly at the same time. And the universe is a tapestry of thought produced by the human mind. This realization indicates that the whole of humankind, including its systems and environment, is merely a creation of consciousness (Heisenberg's Uncertainty Principle).

The primary dynamic of complexity theory indicates that order can be reinforced by comprehending and exploiting the latent structure of deterministic disorder. Order is still of fundamental importance in the new context. Order provides the core stability for survival and existence. Certain types of order must be further

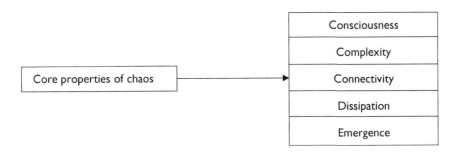

Fig. 1.2. The primary set of properties in complex adaptive systems.

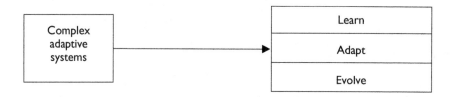

Fig. 1.3. The basic abilities of intelligent complex adaptive systems.

strengthened and enlarged to prolong the existence of a system. This desire can best be achieved by tapping into the innovation and creativity embedded in complexity.

The dynamic between order and disorder is intriguing. It is accepted that the universe as a whole is expanding and hence entropy and disorder are increasing at all moments in time. This phenomenon is captured in the second law of thermodynamics. However, in the midst of chaos, countless centers of order emerge, each serving as a local center for structure and order of different kinds to be created and enforced. Lives and systems of various forms and levels such as human beings, ecosystems and human organizations, are products of this dynamic. All these systems are complex and adaptive in nature.

In complex adaptive systems, the spaces of order are continuously reinforced through exploiting the innovation and creativity of the spaces of complexity. The systems learn, adapt, and evolve in the process. These basic abilities of complex adaptive systems are captured in Fig. 1.3. The emergent dynamic of evolution sustains and prolongs the existence of such systems. Systems that fail to maintain this dynamic dissolve into the mainstream expansion and vanish. Such appearing and disappearing acts are taking place perpetually in the universe.

1.4. Properties of Complex Adaptive Systems

A complex adaptive system comprises a group of dynamically interactive and changing heterogeneous agents. It is an open system in perpetual motion. Even the set of rules governing its dynamic is evolving. New information varies the inputs of the system as it tries to adapt by self-organizing and co-evolving. Its ability to anticipate, respond to, and influence the change in environmental conditions is vital, as a slight variation in initial conditions can lead to a totally unpredictable surface phenomenon. The surface phenomenon may be unpredictable because of the large number of feedback loops in the systems.

Thus, the first important property of such systems is the butterfly effect. Complex adaptive systems can be highly sensitive to initial conditions. A small variation in initial conditions can lead to a totally unpredictable output. Lorenz was the first to observe this interesting property during his weather forecasting computation, which renders weather forecasting beyond a few days meaningless. Apparently, comprehending the butterfly effect is extremely crucial when managing human complex adaptive systems.

The second property of complex adaptive systems is that their present state cannot be measured with absolute accuracy as in a human society. As such systems usually have infinitely large numbers of input points or interacting agents, their evolution trajectories cannot be described accurately, since a complete knowledge of the present state cannot be acquired. This characteristic exists in human organizations too. As the systems are highly sensitive to initial conditions and yet the present state cannot be accurately and completely defined, exact solutions in the form that are commonly understood do not exist. This is a significant observation that leaders and managers of human organizations must learn to handle.

Next, complex adaptive systems are adaptive, that is, they continuously consume new information and react on it. Such systems learn and evolve. Adaptation is a significant property of such systems, and they can only survive if they undergo dissipation and emergence as well. In addition, complex adaptive systems must co-evolve with the environment which itself is usually a composite complex adaptive system. An economy and its businesses demonstrate such a relationship.

As stipulated above, complex adaptive systems comprise both spaces of order and complexity. These systems possess the ability to exploit complexity to reinforce order with the aim of sustaining their existence. Complexity is deterministic disorder and not total chaos. Such a system exhibits aperiodic states similar to the Lorenz attractors. In human organizations, it is also in these spaces of complexity/edge of chaos that innovation and creativity are embedded.

Thus, recognizing the presence of punctuated equilibrium/edge of chaos is extremely significant. Complex adaptive systems are marked by stasis, a stable pattern of activity lasting for a period of time, and disrupted by short periods of rapid changes, known as punctuation points. Punctuated equilibrium makes it difficult for a system that is not adaptive to survive for long. Such a system tends to be complacent during a period of calm and cannot adjust fast enough when the situation turns complex. An adaptive system, on the other hand, is always dynamic, innovative, reactive and even proactive. In this respect, a smart evolver is an emergent strategist.

Finally, complex adaptive systems can be locked in a red queen race. In this situation a competitive advantage can only be sustained for a very short period. Thus, a niche created does not last long. In this environment, the approach to survival is to develop continuously temporary advantages. In the red queen race, the winners are the faster runners. The winning positions must be renewed at all times, and there is no ultimate destination. Being trapped in such a situation does not appear to be too pleasant or comfortable.

1.5. Managing Complex Adaptive Systems

It is now apparent that a complex adaptive system can have infinitely large numbers of points of crisis, each of them with the ability to magnify small changes, as these points are highly unstable. The whole situation appears to be highly complex. At first sight, the sensitive dependence on initial conditions and other characteristics observed seem to render long-term forecasting/strategic planning of human organizations meaningless. Nothing can be accomplished in such a situation.

However, when the output states of complex adaptive systems are examined, the perception is modified. Nonlinear adaptive systems exhibit four different output states, namely, stable, periodic, deterministic aperiodic (strange), and chaotic states (see Fig. 1.4). The complexity theory concentrates on the third state which is complex and yet at the same time deterministic. In this state, the system is at the edge of chaos. Today, the richness of this state is neither fully understood nor exploited.

Fig. 1.4. The four states of complex adaptive systems.

In addition, the variation in output of many complex adaptive systems tends to be small most of the time, with large fluctuations occurring only occasionally. This may be a comforting observation. It indicates that all that have been put in place throughout history is not totally irrelevant or obsolete. Although a change in mindset is essential, the transformation from the past to the future does have some continuity. But extra cautions have to be taken when making the above statement. Destruction/discontinuity occurs at punctuation points. Besides, the current rapidly changing environment indicates that the world and its subsystems are moving into the third state more frequently.

In this respect, to manage complex adaptive systems effectively, a combination of deliberate and emergent strategies must be adopted. During the formulation of deliberate strategy, planning is the key function, forecasting is linear, and accuracy is high. However, when disequilibrium sets in, the emergent component, which emphasizes fast learning, adaptation and evolution, becomes the key approach. In this event, complexity characteristics such as self-organization and bio-diversification may become critical. The integrated new approach in strategic management is illustrated in Fig. 1.5.

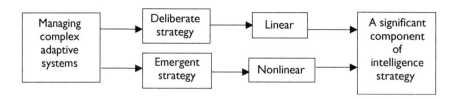

Fig. 1.5. The new management strategy that takes care of both the linear and nonlinear characteristics of complex adaptive systems.

1.6. Edge of Chaos: An Unexplored Goldmine

The recognition that intelligent human organizations are complex adaptive systems stipulates that chaos and complexity theory are new domains that must be better comprehended and effectively utilized. And in complex adaptive systems, the edge of chaos is the most critical territory that must be carefully explored and exploited. Basically, the human thinking systems must be raised to a higher level of consciousness whereby the nuggets embedded at the edge of chaos can be creatively or innovatively used. To date, the edge of chaos has always been avoided by human organizations because of the higher risk involved, that it is foreign, and the current mindset is not prepared to mine it.

So, what is the edge of chaos on the physical perspective? When does an adaptive system move into such a state? What are its characteristics? Nonlinearity and sensitive dependence on initial conditions alone are not enough to create chaotic conditions in systems. Chaos develops in nonlinear systems where the elements are also interdependent on one another. Besides, the nonlinearity of a system manifests itself more explicitly when it is far-from-equilibrium. Far-from-equilibrium means that the system is constantly changing and not returning to some prefixed states. Human organizations are observed to exhibit all the above characteristics (see Fig. 1.6 and the Appendix).

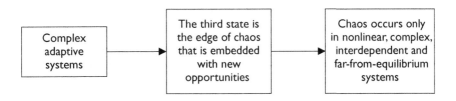

Fig. 1.6. Chaos and edge of chaos in complex adaptive systems.

Thus, the exploration of the edge of chaos requires a redefined mindset with a fresh mental dimension. The human mind must be nurtured to venture into this unexplored, nonlinear, complex and also rich territory. The organizational (societal, corporate) culture must also be supportive to such an endeavor. As the journey can be haphazard, risk-taking and failure must be accepted with a more positive perspective. It must be taken as a learning process. The reward is the huge returns from a small investment when the butterfly effect is activated.

The discussion above vividly indicates that understanding the complexity and nonlinear dynamic of human organizations, and being able to adopt and apply some of the concepts of complexity theory to the management of such systems are crucial in the knowledge-intensive environment. The new comprehension reveals a new direction that human organizations can be managed and organized.

Where chaos begins, classical science stops.

James Gleick, Chaos

II
The New Paradigm

In this chapter, the emergence of a new paradigm is discussed. The new paradigm is the intelligence paradigm which stipulates that organizing around intelligence is the strategy to adopt in the knowledge-intensive environment. The human thinking system and its intelligence forms the focal center of the new theory. This paradigmatic shift in mindset and approach in leading and managing human organizations is significant to everyone.

2.1. Introduction

The human thinking systems are the primary components of all human setups irrespective of their fundamental function (economic, education, social, political or spiritual). The human minds are also the only sources that intense intrinsic intelligence emerges from in this world. Over the past two decades, new developments and challenges have been affecting the thinking systems. Some of the exciting changes that must be noted include the following events:

a. The awareness and knowledge structures of the individual human thinking system have been constantly elevated through better education and knowledge acquisition.

b. Information, a vital input to all human complex adaptive systems that once travels at the speed of horses/planes, now travels at the speed of light.

c. Consequently, the relationships and process dynamic taking place among a group of interacting minds have been drastically modified.

d. Finally, human beings worldwide are more closely connected due to technological advancement, and hence a competitor need not be localized.

2.2. The New Awareness

Associated with the above observations, the current generation of human beings will have to nurture in themselves a new dimension of awareness. The higher level of awareness must encompass the following understanding and abilities:

a. The human thinking systems and their organizations that were once linear and structured (at least perceived to be so) have become nonlinear and more dynamic.

b. Reductionism that worked for simple linear systems does not work for the more complex nonlinear systems.

c. Human organizations that were once machine-like must now be more mind-like.

d. The interdependency among individuals, human organizations, as well as human organizations and their environment has increased substantially.

e. The two mental functions of awareness and mindfulness that emerge from consciousness are equally significant. Although, to date the second function has always been neglected.

f. Intangible assets such as intellectual property and mental capital are now more valuable than traditional economic resources.

2.3. The Fresh Mindset

Inevitably, a totally redefined mindset is essential to understand, exploit and survive in the new knowledge-intensive and fast changing environment. The fresh mindset should constitute a new paradigm that indicates a new direction for individuals to lead, organize, manage and survive comfortably in the new context:

a. Human organizations and its human thinking systems are complex adaptive systems and therefore the current leadership and management philosophy must be transformed.

b. The state of the mind of the interacting agents in the organization must be allocated top priority.

c. An effective relationship among the interacting agents must be carefully cultivated and constantly reinforced.

d. Human organizations must be organized around intelligence, and equipped with an intense intelligence source and an equivalent of the central nervous system.

e. Human organizations must be nurtured and handled like biological beings, as intelligent organizations process collective intelligence and behave like intelligent corporate beings.

f. Complexity, nonlinearity and interdependency cannot be ignored. Instead, these properties must be exploited.

g. Similarly, the core properties of chaos, consciousness, complexity, connectivity, dissipation and emergence must be more deeply scrutinized and effectively used. New opportunities are embedded at the edge of chaos.

2.4. The Intelligence Paradigm

The central theme of this fresh recognition clearly points towards the significance of developing an intelligence paradigm (illustrated in Fig. 2.1). The new paradigm indicates that the individual mind and intelligence must be the center of analysis and experimentation. Thus, organizing around intelligence is the best option for nurturing intelligent organizations. The new priority on managing human organizations is on the better management of the human thinking systems and their nonlinear dynamic. The intrinsic intelligence and knowledge structures in the individual minds must be more effectively utilized by the organization.

In an intelligent organization, an orgmind has to be nurtured too. It is from the orgmind and the intangible deep structure that the physical structure evolves (see Fig. 2.2). Thus, in the new environment, leaders and managers of human organizations must examine

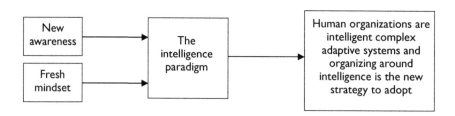

Fig. 2.1. The new paradigm for leading, managing and structuring human organizations.

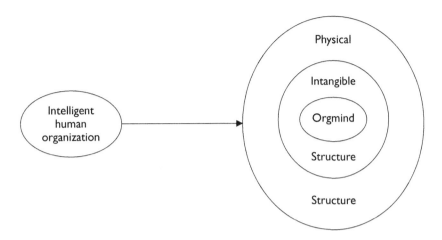

Fig. 2.2. The basic structure of an intelligent human organization.

and search beyond the physical structure. They must immerse themselves into the intangible structure and the orgmind to better understand and exploit the mysterious power of intelligence and collective intelligence.

Thus, the new paradigm also focuses on elevating the collective intelligence, enhancing the quality of connectivity, and exploiting the bio-logic aspect of human organizations. Inherently, group features such as organizational learning, corporate knowledge structure, adaptation and emergence are new areas of concern. In this respect, an effective human organization in the new era must be an intelligent complex adaptive system that can create and exploit complexity and nonlinearity like intelligent biological organisms.

Apparently, the paradigmatic shift in mindset calls for a new theory for leadership, management and business operations. This new theory of human organization encompassing the social, economic and political domains is the intelligent organization theory.

It is significant for all individuals who wish to be an effective member of the new global society to comprehend and exploit this theory well. This theory provides a more holistic view of the human thinking systems and their interactive dynamic in human organizations. In particular, leaders of human organizations, whether they are top business executives, political leaders, or social/welfare/education administrators must nurture this fresh mindset to remain relevant for the future.

Without the randomness of chaos, the rich variety and diversity of evolution would be stifled and throttled. Chaos is the rich soil from which creativity is born.

Uri Merry, Coping with Uncertainty

III
Fundamentals of Intelligent Organization Theory

The foundation of the intelligent organization theory is conceptualized in this chapter. The significance of intelligence and organizing around intelligence is discussed. The roles of intelligence, information and language in a human organization are examined. The necessity of nurturing an effective intelligence enhancer encompassing three entities, namely, intelligence, knowledge and theory in the human thinking system is proposed. The basic aspects of the deliberate strategy and emergent strategy are further examined. The above concepts are developed with respect to the fact that the human mind and human organizations are complex adaptive systems.

3.1. Introduction

As indicated in the earlier two chapters, the human mind is the "epicenter" of all human setups, and the mind and orgmind are complex adaptive systems. In this respect, all human organizations are also composite complex adaptive systems. The basic elements of these systems, human beings, interact with one another and form the feedback loops. Any one member of an organization can have a direct or indirect influence on another member. The influence from a message communicated is very often under-reacted or over-reacted upon. Thus, human group behavior is not simply the sum of the individual behavior. Hence, the dynamic and the outcomes of human interactions include a nonlinear dimension.

Inevitably, in the emerging environment, human organizations are behaving and evolving as intelligent corporate beings. The economy is its ecological system. Similar to biological entities, human organizations embrace the abilities of learning, evolving and competing. The intrinsic force driving the above dynamic is intelligence. And higher levels of intelligence are manifested as sophisticated information processing abilities. Conversely, any system that possesses a structure is embedded with information. Consequently, understanding intelligence, information processing, knowledge structure, and quality connectivity is a key to understanding the orgmind.

3.2. Intelligence and Intelligent Traits

Intelligence is the primary entity that enables a biological being to compete for survival, to undergo evolution, and to save its species from extinction. The presence of intelligence allows the organism to interact with its environment and to make adjustments to itself. The act of adaptation, evolution and emergence is a key to survival in nature. The same basic principles also ensure that human organizations survive and compete better in the new knowledge-based economy. On a broader perspective, all the five core properties of chaos, namely, consciousness, connectivity, complexity, dissipation and emergence must be constantly reflected upon.

So what is intelligence? Intelligence is a mental ability: it is the power of perceiving, learning, understanding and knowing. Such a definition of intelligence is closely associated with consciousness. It may be interesting to determine at what level of intelligence consciousness emerges. This is a puzzle of the mind that the mind itself cannot consciously resolve. It is a mystery that has pre-occupied some of the best minds for centuries. A school of thought believes that this mystery can never be resolved because it is beyond the capability of a physical network that has something on the order of billions of neurons. It is a structural constraint. Perhaps even a multi-trillion-neuron network is required to unveil the secret.

In the intelligent organization theory, intelligence is perceived to be an intangible entity similar to energy in the sciences and technologies. It is invisible, intangible, and at the moment, not easily quantifiable. But its presence can be felt. Its status is similar to energy a century ago. It is the existence of intelligence as an entity that enables intelligent traits to be manifested. It is the presence of this entity that allows intelligent mental abilities such as information processing, knowledge structuring and perception to be manifested and executed. The economic capability of an intelligent being is also fuelled by the same entity. This fundamental concept is stated as the first axiom of the theory:

Axiom I
There exists an intangible entity known as intelligence in all intelligent systems that provides the fundamental driving force for all their cognition functions and other activities.

In this sense, there exists a relationship between awareness and intelligence. However, the exact formula of the relationship is unknown. As higher levels awareness are associated with higher levels intelligence, the presence of an intense intelligence source is significant. An intense intelligence source is needed to generate higher levels intelligence. Physically, a dense and well-connected network with an enormous number of neurons must be present to create and sustain the strange phenomenon. The above observation leads to the first postulation:

Postulate I

A necessary condition for higher levels intelligence to exist is the presence of a sufficiently intense intelligence source.

The absence of the intense source indicates the absence of human-level or second-order consciousness. A feeble source or an intelligence web is not able to generate the same level of awareness. Lower level consciousness, mainly raw sensations or qualia are not very useful by themselves. In this respect, a colony of ants is only an intelligence web, and its activities can never flourish beyond its present status, unless an intense intelligence source emerges. The weakly connected network of an ant nest is not sufficiently intense. This recognition is stipulated as the second postulate:

Postulate II

The presence of an intelligence web is a necessary but not a sufficient condition for generating higher levels mental activities and second-order consciousness.

However, the presence of an intelligent web in a living organism is significant because it is this internal network which allows intelligence to be transmitted from the intense intelligence source to the other parts of the organism, and vice versa. Such a web is also an internal information action and reaction system. It forms a vital communication structure in all intelligent beings.

The tangible component of the web is the physical network that supports the communication of information, decisions, and other intelligent-related entities. The network comprises intelligent nodes that can be both natural and constructed. Therefore, knowledge bases and other artificial intelligent systems are also part of the web. The manner in which the nodes communicate among themselves, the types of information that flow between two nodes, the effectiveness and efficiency of the network, and ultimately the level of intelligence of the web, are some major concerns when nurturing the internal structure.

An extension of the web is an environment scanning and responding component. Any intelligent system that learns, adapts and evolves must possess such a component. Otherwise, it is literally dead and consciousness does not exist. It is then no different from a crystal or a snowflake that contains only proto-intelligence. The requirement indicates that a system is highly intelligent only if it is open and continuously interacting with its environment. Although, it must be added at this juncture that highly intelligent beings usually do lots of internal search, a mental function known as mindfulness.

The environment scanning and responding component must possess certain characteristics before it can be regarded as functioning intelligently. Some of the essential features include the following abilities:

a. To scan and detect environmental signals coming from environmental targets.

b. To process the environmental signals locally or to transmit them to the intense intelligence source for a decision.

c. To respond to the environmental signals.

d. To introduce changes, and thus have the ability to influence the environmental targets.

With respect to a business organization, some environmental targets are its customers, suppliers, competitors, and related government institutions. The environmental functions are to detect, evaluate, respond and change. And the target functions are sensing, influencing, buying, selling, competing, and entering into an alliance with another organization. The third postulate, listed below, captures the existence of the environment interacting component as an important subsystem of an intelligent organization:

Postulate III

The presence of an environment scanning and responding component is a necessary requirement for the continuous survival and evolution of an intelligent system.

Thus, the physical structure of an intelligent organization must possess the following three features (see Fig. 3.1):

a.   An intense intelligence source.

b.   An intelligence web that spreads and permeates the entire system.

c.   An environment scanning and responding component.

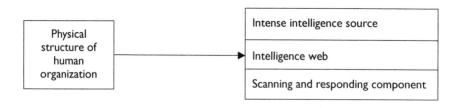

Fig. 3.1. The physical intelligent network of human organization.

3.3. Levels of Organizational Intelligence

Although intelligence is manifested as a continuous spectrum in nature, constructing a conceptual structure containing different intelligence levels renders the analysis of intelligent human systems more comprehensible. In this model, a four-level structure is conceived. And each level is defined by certain unique characteristics as follows:

a. *Level 0 Intelligence: Slavery*
    An organizational system operating at this level is only capable of economic production. It has literally no intelligence capability and has no environment scanning and responding component. It is a non-thinking, purely mechanistic system. It behaves like a slave whose intelligence is suppressed. As far as the intelligence domain is concerned, the system is dumb. A mechanical machine exists in this state.

b. *Level I Intelligence: Instinctive*
    Besides economic production, a system in this case is capable of sensing simple changes in the environment, such as changes in demand, and responds by varying the quantity of its output. The behavior of such a system is instinctive. Its level of intelligence is low. Many business organizations, at the moment, exist in this state, similar to plants in an ecological system. There is not much "mobility" in this state.

c. *Level II Intelligence: Survival Seeking*
    A system can be classified in this category if an attempt has been made to improve its environment scanning and responding component. Such a system is also aware of the significance of having a well-established intelligence web. It is increasingly reactive to changes, and has assimilated learning and adaptive capabilities. It is a mobile intelligent being.

d. *Level III Intelligence: Highly Intelligent*
A system in this category has a sophisticated intelligent network. It is highly reactive, as well as proactive to the environment. It is intelligent enough to influence the environment to enhance its existence. Whenever possible and necessary, this option is exercised. Such a system can diversify, "migrate" and have "offspring". Thus, existing in this state, the system possesses its own orgmind and collective intelligence, and behaves as a highly intelligent biological being.

3.4. Intelligence, Information and Language

It has been recognized that any system which exhibits structure contains information. The more intricately organized a system is, the more information has accumulated within that system. This statement stipulates that a more organized system contains more structured information or knowledge, and hence possesses a higher level of intelligence. A piece of crystal contains proto-intelligence but it is non-living. An ant colony is an intelligence web but an ant cannot survive on its own. However, a human being that possesses an intense intelligence source has the capability of creating awareness and also has better capability of individual learning and survival.

In all circumstances, data are useful only with respect to a context, that is, data must be transformed into useful information when the necessity for consumption arises. The ways in which a set of information is structured, communicated and utilized further determine its usefulness. Besides, certain relationships must be established between a set of information and an existing knowledge structure. When a set of information is consumed, the knowledge structure is altered, and internalization is said to have taken place in the mind. Data and information in this respect are also entities of a physical symbol system and they collectively form a language.

Underlying and quietly forging the thinking process is the presence of such a language. Without the existence of a language, human thinking activities would be simplistic, and human civilizations would not have flourished to their present levels. "Without language our mental capacities would be poor indeed, comparable to those of the higher animals" (Einstein, 1954: p. 13). The processing of pictorial signals and sound signals would not have the same level of sophistication and dynamism as manipulating a physical symbol system. There seems to be an association among the number of neurons present within an intelligence source and its ability to manipulate and to create abstract concepts using a physical symbol system.

In operation, a piece of information is simply expressed as a linear combination of some characters in a physical symbol system. Communicating a concept is a more complex process. If the language used to transmit the concept is linear, some richness in ideas may be lost during communication. "A language rooted in a linear, mechanistic view of the universe creates different actions and opportunities from a language that emerges from a complex intelligent view of the universe" (McMaster, 1996: p. 32).

In fact, the relationships among information, knowledge, concept, and the language used to create and communicate them are intriguing, if not mystical. Masters speak differently from others in their discipline. When people attain a certain level of mastery, it is not merely their words that are different, but also the meaning of their words, and their understanding of their existence. A single word or a short collection of statements can convey a very deep thought or meaning.

In a human organization, language is the medium that helps to facilitate the dynamic of the intangible component of the intelligent structure. It penetrates and flows through the web and binds the organization. The automatic behavior and thinking of a human organization is made possible by language. A change in the ways of speaking and thinking will change its coherence and competitiveness.

A change in the language of interpretation will generate new information from existing data. The new information may be crucial. Engagement, a critical activity in all human-related setups, is made possible by the presence of a language.

Therefore, a human organization must create a conscientious effort to ensure that its level of interpretation using language is more advanced and sophisticated than that of its rivals. The exact communication between any two nodes in the web, the meaning of the language used, the more subtle interpretation of the language used, are areas for repetitive scrutiny. In this respect, the long-neglected role of language operating in the deep conceptual structure of human organizations must be re-examined. This binding medium must be better understood. The above discussion leads to the proposal of the fourth postulate:

Postulate IV
The survival of an intelligent system is highly dependent on the awareness, connectivity and coherence of the orgmind and intangible deep structure. An optimal physical structure can only emerge from a highly intelligent intangible structure. The physical structure cannot be created and sustained artificially without a firm intangible structure as its foundation.

3.5. Theory and Knowledge Structure

Evolving from the physical to the conceptual use of a physical symbol system, within a certain domain, a theory arises. A theory is a set of statements which allows an intelligent being self-examination. It is a reference source for internal searching. In addition, a theory also serves as an analytical lens that enables the intelligent system to examine its environment and the events happening in it. Without a theory, there is no proper basis for analyses and explanations. A thought that emerges without such a basis may not be very valuable. Therefore, a theory is an intelligence enabler.

A theory is not and cannot be stagnant. It emerges and evolves with time. In many instances, it has never been fully explicit or understood, even if its fundamentals may be well established and widely practised by the community that adopts it. However, to understand the logic of a theory, and to use it consciously as an analytical lens, is a new mindset that is critically needed to enhance intelligence.

In addition, a new theory drives leadership. Leadership is meaningless without a theory to support its mission. When a person leads, a theory helps to explain his/her leadership by clearly indicating the direction and intention. Theory is a compass indicating the direction in which to steer. In fact, a theory also helps to ensure that an intention and its actions are coherent, and such a match is vital for any human organization to compete successfully.

A theory is not necessarily abstract—it is not always a "theory of relativity". In reality, an operational theory can be fairly simple. As mentioned, quite often people use theories without realizing their existence and importance. Such theories are subconsciously built up in the mind and can be relatively simple. However, it is much more beneficial if a theory is well understood, made explicit, and fully supported by the group. Its presence must be known and accepted before the theory can be exploited effectively. The existence of theory in intelligent systems is stated as the next axiom:

Axiom II
There exist one or more theories in all intelligent systems that serve as the compass and analytical lens for the systems.

It is through a theory that information is consumed and added on to a knowledge structure. A knowledge structure is a large-scale accumulation of related pieces of information over a long period of time. When a piece of information is consumed by a thinking system, it alters the knowledge structure of the system. The consequence of a decision-making process is influenced by internalized knowledge structures. In this respect, a knowledge structure is another intelligence enabler.

Therefore, the presence of quality knowledge structures in intelligent systems is essential and crucial. Such structures are the products of prolonged intelligent-related activities. When pieces of information are manipulated and consumed, a knowledge structure capturing the relationships of the pieces will gradually emerge, if sufficient time and effort have been invested. These structures are also reference sources when further pieces of information are brought into the thinking system. The next axiom on knowledge structures is stated below:

Axiom III
There exist one or more internalized knowledge structures in all intelligent systems that are the reference sources for intelligent activities and actions.

In this regard, knowledge structures, theories and intelligence are constantly enriching each other in an intelligent system. These three entities form an intelligent enabler triad. The triad is the intelligence enhancer of the mind and orgmind. The presence of such an enhancer in the human thinking systems is vital. It is the most significant dynamo that drives complex thinking in highly intelligent systems. The dynamic of the intelligence enhancer is

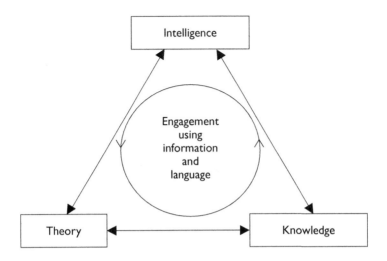

Fig. 3.2. The intelligence enhancer of the human thinking system.

illustrated in Fig. 3.2. The functions of this enhancer will be more deeply examined in subsequent chapters.

3.6. Inherent Intelligent Structure and Intelligence Strategy

Designing around intelligence is a creation of nature. It is an inherent feature of the universe and all its microcosms that exhibit stability. As mentioned earlier, in the sea of chaotic expansion, infinite numbers of "bubbles of order" proliferate. The centers of these bubbles are the "local order centers". In the vicinity of each of these centers is a space of order. A space of order is a region of established structure and stability, where activities constantly reduce entropy, and relationships are linear. The characteristics of such a space are significant to humankind as their predictability provides confidence, comfort and certainty.

However in a space of order, intelligence is not optimized. Information use is rigid and information redundancy is not acceptable or carefully avoided. Its dynamic is linear and usually simplistic. Consequently, creativity and innovation are unconsciously suppressed. For an intelligent organization to prolong its existence, its spaces of order have to be constantly strengthened and enhanced. Thus, venturing beyond order into the unfamiliar territories of complexity is the best option to achieve the above objective.

Just beyond a space of order is a space of complexity. This mysterious sphere is embedded with new unexplored opportunities. The main attributes guiding activities in the space of complexity are intelligence and intense complex information processing. Its characteristics can be nonlinear and the butterfly effect can manifest itself. Nature frequently exploits the dynamism of complexity to support its evolutionary dynamics. In such a space, matter can exist in a state in between solid and liquid, for instance.

Currently, human organizations either have not realized the existence of complexity or have avoided this uncertain space. Operating within the spaces of order has always been the norm. However, confining organizational activities to spaces of order can only sustain survival for a limited period of time. Niches cannot be easily found in territories that are commonly understood. The complexity spaces are the unexplored goldmines. Anyone that is able to recognize new order and structure in complexity acquires an intelligence advantage.

However, the present machine-oriented structure of human organizations suppresses the analysis and exploitation of the spaces of complexity. The structure of the spaces of order of a mechanistic setup is unnatural, as it does not take on a form congruous with biological systems that inherently support their own growth and survival by reaping benefits from the spaces of complexity. The common existing practice of fitting human beings into a machine setup is also not a natural process.

Therefore, the intelligence strategy has to be adopted. Human organizations must ensure that their structure does not end abruptly at the edge of order. Intelligent human systems must venture into the spaces of complexity to reap the latent benefits. In general, structure fluidity, information redundancy, knowledge enhancement and nonlinear use of intelligence, are some of the main characteristics that the new environment requires. These characteristics are some of the key life-supporting features of biological evolutionary systems.

The intelligent organization theory stipulates that human organizations designed around intelligence are more adaptive and competitive. At the center of the deep structure is the orgmind of the organization and embedded in it is its consciousness. The level of consciousness determines the level of collective intelligence and orgmindfulness of the system. Orgmindfulness and collective intelligence, in turn, are responsible for the connectivity of the system. It is only when an organization is orgmindful of its existence before that system can be well connected. Thought technology can play a significant role in this domain.

The connectivity of an organization is determined by its mode of communication. Coherent thought is the social and psychological gel that binds human beings together, and it helps human organizations to achieve functional cohesion. As discussed above, language facilitates engagement and the flow of information, and binds the interacting agents. Language also allows for more abstract and intense interaction. Very often, concepts can only be successfully explained using language. In addition, language also enhances the linguistic act of interpretation. Therefore, language is a major concern when nurturing the deep structure, and when extending the boundaries of the spaces of complexity. Without a highly developed language, the intelligence enhancer cannot function at a higher level of complexity. Language facilitates the interaction among the three entities in the enhancer. In this respect, language and collective intelligence are closely associated.

In the new theory, an intelligent business organization that is constantly learning, responding to the environment, and adapting and evolving with time will not adopt a stagnant five-year strategic plan. As the internal and external parameters change, an intelligent system will have to adjust or even transform its orgmind, intelligence enhancer, deep structure and surface structure, accordingly. Inevitably, its strategic plan will have to be altered or updated constantly. A transformation may even be a necessity depending on the acceleration and complication of the change involved.

Basically, the deliberate strategy commonly adopted today is useful only when the environment is stable or fairly predictable. However, when the environment becomes highly dynamic and the future cannot be well predicted, an emergent strategy is more viable. In this case, the scan– respond–evolve cycle will have to be exploited frequently or even continuously. In reality, as order and complexity always co-exist, a combination of the two strategies is essential. A combination of deliberate and emergent strategies is a more viable option in the new context. Some differences in the two strategies are summarized in Table 3.1.

Finally, it must be emphasized again that recognizing the presence of punctuated equilibrium is a new awareness that today's managers,

Table 3.1. Some differences between deliberate strategy and emergent strategy.

Deliberate Strategy	Emergent Strategy
Presence of planned intention	Absence of planned intention
Destination and environment are highly predictable	Destination and environment cannot be well-predicted
Path of advancement can be charted	Path of advancement emerges gradually
A plan exists	A plan emerges
The plan is usually centrally formulated	Formulation requires broad consensus
The plan is implemented with high precision	Implementation requires high degree of tolerance

social scientists, economists and political leaders must acquire. Punctuated equilibrium makes it difficult for a system that is not adaptive to survive for long. Such a system that tends to be complacent during a period of calm cannot adjust when the situation turns complex. An adaptive system, on the other hand, is always dynamic, innovative, creative and proactive. In this respect, a smart evolver is an emergent strategist.

3.7. Conclusion

It may be beneficial to summarize the foundation of the intelligent organization theory that has been proposed before concluding this chapter. The most basic concepts that have been discussed are as follows:

a. Human organizations are intelligent beings.

b. They are corporate beings with an orgmind and collective intelligence.

c. Their level of intelligence can be elevated through proper design.

d. The more intelligent an organization, the more adaptive and competitive it is.

e. Such a competitive advantage is an intelligence advantage.

Therefore, there exists a critical relationship between intelligence and human organizations, as there exists a similar relationship between intelligence and biological organisms. The requirements of this vital connection are summarized below:

a. The presence of an intense intelligence source is vital; otherwise, the activities of organizational systems will have no proper co-ordination and direction.

b. The existence of a sophisticated environment scanning and responding component is essential because such a component not only enables organizations to interact with their environment, but also enables organizations to elevate their collective intelligence.

c. The spread and integration of the intelligence web with the economic production functions connecting the components specified in (a) and (b), is a necessity in business organizations as the absence of the web indicates that that organization is paralyzed.

d. The flexible physical structure must be supported by an intelligent deep process structure. An intelligent and coherent orgmind is the fundamental intelligent stratum of all intelligent organizations.

In addition, it is important to recognize that the collective intelligence in human organizations can be elevated through proper design. Some benefits derived from organizing around intelligence are as follows:

a. The intelligence strategy that focuses on an intelligence-oriented design helps to elevate the collective intelligence and competitive level of human organizations.

b. This new designing approach allows human organizations to settle more spontaneously into a competitive state that is closer to an inherent intelligent structure of nature.

c. Human organizations with an intelligent structure possess an orgmind, a deep intangible structure and a surface structure. Such intelligent systems are more coherent with information and knowledge-related functions, and therefore they survive better in the knowledge-intensive environment.

d. Intelligent human organizations are more adaptive to both linear and orderly changes, as well as nonlinear and complex changes. Therefore, such organizations adopt both the deliberate and emergent strategies. In this respect, intelligent organizations are smarter evolvers.

Aggregation of complex adaptive systems into a composite complex adaptive system is an effective way to open up new level of organization. The composite system then consists of adaptive agents constructing schemata to account for and deal with one another's behavior.

Murray Gell-Mann, The Quark and the Jaguar

IV
Basic Structure of Intelligent Human Organization

In this chapter, the general structure of an intelligent human organization is further discussed. Some characteristics of intelligent biological organisms and other complex adaptive systems are scrutinized and compared with human organizations as composite complex adaptive systems. It is crucial for intelligent human organizations to possess these characteristics for more effective competition in the new complex environment. In particular, the characteristics of collective intelligence, orgmindfulness and connectivity are examined.

4.1. Introduction

It is now understood that intelligent human organizations are complex adaptive systems that possess spaces of order and spaces of complexity (see Fig. 4.1). A space of order is linear and its events are more easily understood. This space provides predictability, comfort, and confidence. However, operating in a space of this nature can only sustain survival for a limited period of time. Niches cannot be easily found in a territory that is commonly understood and exploited. Competitive human organizations will have to endeavor beyond order.

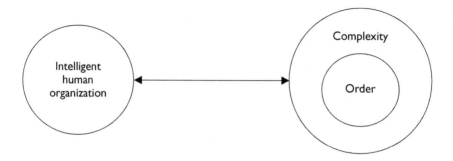

Fig. 4.1. Order and complexity co-exist in all human organizations.

Innovation and creativity are more abundantly deposited in the spaces of complexity where activities are nonlinear. Because of their nonlinearity, the complexity spaces contain an enormous amount of unexplored knowledge. Anyone that is able to discern some structures in these spaces early possesses an intelligence advantage. In the event of comprehending a portion of a space of complexity, the knowledge derived can be used to strengthen and enlarge the spaces of order. In the process, the opportunities of the organization are broadened. The organization can then move on to explore other portions of the complexity spaces more extensively. Basically, the idea is to tap into and exploit the innovation and creativity of deterministic disorder to further strengthen the structure of order. This cyclical process continually elevates the competitiveness of the organization. It is an evolutionary dynamic that can only be sustained by a high level of collective intelligence.

Physically, the spaces of complexity are perceived to encompass the spaces of order. In reality, the two sets of spaces are intertwined in a complicated manner and "sophisticated" intelligence is required to identify their boundaries. Conscientious effort must be invested to identify the boundaries of these two sets of highly dynamic spaces. Nonetheless, as the benefits derived from understanding and exploiting the complexity spaces is enormous, competitive organizations will still continuously channel resources into the complexity spaces to sustain their competitiveness.

4.2. Structuring Around Intelligence

The primary focal centers of the intelligent organization theory are the mind and orgmind as they are the origins of thought and action. A thought originates in the mind and an action is initiated by a thought. When there is no thought, there is no action. Thus, a more mindful mind is perceived to exercise a better course of action and hence is more intelligent. On the same note, the best means to enhance the collective intelligence of organizations is to concentrate on the connectivity of the intrinsic intelligence sources. Human organizations can elevate their orgmindfulness by focusing on connecting the thoughts of the individual minds. An orgmindful organization is concern about the state of the mind of its interacting agents.

Human minds are nonlinear systems and they are the basic elements of an orgmind. In the new perspective, an organization as a unique single entity is perceived to behave as an evolving intelligent corporate being driven by its own collective intelligence that originates from its orgmind. Similar to biological entities, organizations are able to learn, adapt, compete and evolve with time. As indicated earlier, the intrinsic energy driving the above characteristics is primarily human intelligence. And higher levels of intelligence are best manifested as sophisticated information processing or symbol manipulation abilities.

Thus, as the world moves into the intelligence era, organizations must first discern the primary importance of intelligence and the existence of an orgmind in their setup. An organization must be designed with a structure that allows its own orgmind and collective intelligence to grow. Ideally, it should possess a structure that continually accumulates and internalizes knowledge, and allows its corporate theories and philosophy to evolve with time. Simultaneously, the orgmind would then be expanded and consolidated. In this respect, an orgmind is different from a human mind. The former can be enlarged and its collective intelligence can be elevated substantially.

A key factor to take note of is connectivity. Connectivity in an organization does not simply imply uniformity and homogeneity. The secret embedded here may be unity through diversity, that is, establishing connectivity by accommodating diversification. In this respect, when organizations are structured around intelligence, a new technology that can be exploited is thought technology. This technology focuses on the connectivity of the orgmind and the intangible aspect of the organization. Although putting in place an effective physical structure is important, the underlying dynamic in the deep structure that makes the tangible structure work coherently is even more significant. In an ideal situation, the deep structure should provide the foundation for an intelligent and flexible surface structure to be established.

Primarily, orchestrating the growth and ensuring the coherence of the intangible structure originates from the orgmind. At the moment, few organizations actually place sufficient attention on the orgmind and their intangible structure. Those that have artificially erected their physical structure should recognize that their structural components are not synchronized. An artificially enforced structure can never come close to optimal performance if the intangible structure is weak and divided. Therefore, an understanding of the connectivity of the intrinsic sources, collective intelligence, information processing and knowledge management, is the key to comprehending the orgmind. The above discussion is summarized in Fig. 4.2.

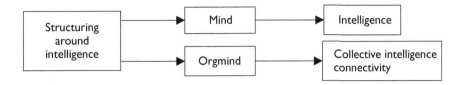

Fig. 4.2. The vital entities to focus on when nurturing a human organization around intelligence.

4.3. Intelligent Interacting Agents

Human beings are the heterogeneous interacting agents that constitute all human organizations. They behave and interact non-linearly. When they form a human organization, they do so with a specific mission in mind, such as economic production or the provision of welfare services. Irrespective of the mission, the organization incorporated is an open system because such a system interacts with the environment, and the agents can enter and leave the system.

The exact patterns of adaptation and evolution of the individuals cannot be predicted in advance. Those that do not or cannot adapt to the group dynamic will leave. And those that can adapt evolve with the system. The whole phenomenon is emergent in nature. Several evolutionary activities such as self-organization, bio-diversification and co-evolution can be unfolding concurrently.

The individual human thinking system, the mind, is a complex adaptive system that possesses linear and nonlinear components. Each mind is extremely complex and must be managed professionally and carefully. In this respect, every mind is a vital factor that can decide whether the organization will succeed or disintegrate.

The dynamic of the mind, being nonlinear, is highly sensitive to initial conditions, and understanding how the mind thinks and interacts is highly significant to intelligent organizations. In this respect, comprehending the properties and functions of the human thinking systems is a necessity. Apparently the most fundamental complex adaptive system in human organizations, the human mind, must be understood first, before the higher level complex adaptive systems can be effective.

An important strategy in the new mindset is getting the individual mind to be mindful first. To be mindful is to be more aware of itself, its internal state. It is a self-reflection function. The intention is to ensure that the mind is in better control of its decisions and actions. The higher the level of mindfulness of the mind, the greater is its ability to manage itself and solve problems. In practice, nurturing this process is by no means a simple task.

A high level of mindfulness can only be attained through conscientious effort. The mind must continuously and perpetually search itself. It must over time build up a set of theories that facilitates coherent thought. There is no shortcut to this endeavor. Concentration is needed to achieve a well-focused mind, and concentrated calmness and clarity are needed to promote better understanding and decision making. The entire process is smooth and soothing only if there is a high level of mindfulness. The decision and action that emerge from such a mental state are different.

To cultivate such a mind the individuals must first be aware of their thoughts. Watching their thoughts increases mindfulness. As a thought begins in the mind, it is at the source, the mind, that it must be checked. The persistent practice of watching helps to avoid interferences by revealing the errors in thoughts at an early stage. In this way, inappropriate actions can also be avoided. The same process also helps to identify new opportunities. Thus, the individuals must mind the mind, and not allow it to drift in the

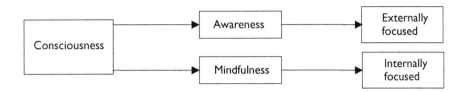

Fig. 4.3. Awareness and mindfulness are the primary mental functions that arise from consciousness.

wrong direction. This is the basic criterion that must be achieved in mind cultivation (see Fig. 4.3).

4.4. Orgmind and Orgmindfulness

In a human organization, the orgmind at the least embraces the minds of all its members. An effective orgmind needs all members of the organization to voluntarily connect their minds to form the pivotal portion of the organizational structure. They are bound due to their own volition. There must be no coercing. Intangibly, it may appear to be the fusion of the individual minds into the orgmind.

As discussed earlier, the state of the individual minds has a profound effect on the orgmind. And the state of the orgmind is not a linear combination of the individual minds. Certain synergetic effects can only be achieved if the individual minds are connected in the right manner. Therefore, the integration of all the intrinsic intelligence sources into one collective source is a tricky endeavor. There may be more than one possible combination. It is a difficult task that leaders and managers have to learn to handle.

However, once that "collective" stage is attained, the organization's concern becomes the full concern of the individual members.

The organization's survival is perceived to be connected to their survival. Thus, nurturing a well-connected orgmind must be another top priority and accomplishment of an intelligent organization.

Once an orgmind is established, orgmindfulness must be further enhanced. It can be attained in the same manner as nurturing individual mindfulness, although the task involved here is more delicate. The attributes of a well-focused, clear, calm and well-controlled mind also apply to organizations. A drifting and disintegrated orgmind is disastrous. An organization that aims to exploit the intelligence-based paradigm must attain a high level of orgmindfulness. Only when the orgmind is highly orgmindful is the organization ready to adopt other intelligence-related re-structuring (see Fig. 4.4).

If a mind exists within the body, logically it ought to thoroughly comprehend the internal environment of its body first. Very often, human beings tend to be more attracted by external events. Many organizations are observed to have the same traits. Focusing internally, in particular, on the intangible dynamic is an important aspect that is always neglected. It must be emphasized that an organization must direct its attention internally first if it is to achieve a high level of collective intelligence. By constantly and conscientiously removing or dissipating extra entropy from the deep structure, the organization is in a better position to face a battle as a united entity.

The primary reason for the failure of some organizations is the absence of an effective orgmind. In other cases, it is the deterioration

Fig. 4.4. The crucial characteristics of the orgmind.

of the orgmind that causes the collapse of these organizations. Very often, failed businesses are not directly eliminated by other businesses. If an organization is alert and orgmindful, and does constant internal searches, its chance of survival is high. On the other hand, if its orgmind is chaotic or brain-dead, it does not have to be destroyed by others; rather, it self-destructs.

4.5. Intelligent Intangible Structure

At the core of the organizational structure is the orgmind of the organization. The level of consciousness of the orgmind is responsible for its overall performance. Consciousness and connectivity are two mutually enforcing properties. It is only when an organization is highly conscious of its existence and activities, and well connected structurally, that learning and adaptation can emerge successfully. Such an intelligent structure will lead to a tremendous improvement in decision-making and evolution. Only then can an organization be collectively perceived as a single unique entity.

The focus on the structure of organizations is due to one fundamental belief. The capacity of the structure limits their growth and competitiveness. Thus, the structural dynamics of organizations determine their potential for successful evolution. Inevitably, over time, such systems move towards the edge of chaos. At the edge of chaos, these organizations have two options: either face disintegration because of stagnation or move into a higher order of complexity. An organization that has consciously nurtured its collective intelligence has a higher probability of achieving a better order of existence.

In general, organizations must be able to evolve into optimal states similar to, for instance, the evolution of the ape family into different species, which takes place spontaneously by optimizing the dynamic of the orgmind, the intangible structure and the physical structure. These species have their differences and commonalties.

Fig. 4.5. The crucial characteristics of the intangible structure.

Each species exists in its present state due to a set of intrinsic factors and its interaction with the environment over time. Therefore, it is crucial that organizations be able to evolve in this manner, too. To identify an appropriate equilibrium state quickly is a pivotal necessity. However, the state of equilibrium of each organization is different, depending on its internal dynamic, structure and environment. In addition, the state of equilibrium itself is a dynamic equilibrium and not a static one.

A derivation of this theory is the concept of humanizing organizations. This development is by no means a coincidence. In an intelligence-focused environment, the humanizing of organizations is a parallel development, as human beings cannot be treated as machine parts. In the new socio-economic and political environment, human beings must be treated as human beings again. The humanization of an organization emphasizes trust, respect and other human-sensitive attributes. A large layer of the intangible structure, a web of human attributes, has to be highly regarded. Only then can quality connectivity and a supportive culture be nurtured, as illustrated in Fig. 4.5. This highly desired trait can only be achieved if a high level of collective intelligence and orgmindfulness emerge from the core of interacting human minds.

4.6. Intelligent Physical Structure

As stipulated earlier, it is vital that the architectural setup of the surface structure should emerge from the deep structure. Such a process is evolutionary in nature. When the deep structure is changed gradually, the surface is also altered, but not vice-versa. So altering the organizational chart and hoping that the culture of the organization will be changed will never materialize. Such a dynamic is not sustainable. Thus, time and effort must be invested into nurturing the intangible structure. It is only when the deep structure supports the surface structure it helps to create, that an organization becomes more nimble, flexible, adaptive and intelligent.

The physical structure itself is also extremely significant. This is the structure that we are constantly in contact with during our daily operations. In general, the nervous system of the physical structure of an intelligent organization possesses three features, namely, an intense intelligence source (organization brain), an environment scanning and responding component, and an intelligence web. The existence of an intense intelligence source is the pivotal factor that distinguishes higher levels intelligent systems from others. The absence of such a source indicates the absence of the leadership node. An intelligent organization cannot compete without proper co-ordination and direction, and this role is initiated and performed by the intense intelligence source.

The intelligence web that spreads and permeates the entire system has its own significance and value. For biological organisms, this web is the nervous system that spreads from the brain. In business organizations, this web must also spread from the intense source, intertwine with, and support the economic production system. In human organizations, the relationship between the web and the intense source is more delicate. In certain instances, the demarcation may not be clear. In addition, extra precautions are necessary to balance the roles of the two components; otherwise, evolutionary characteristics and creativity may be suppressed.

A highly intelligent system has to be responsive to its environment. It must act, react and think like an intelligent biological entity.

Therefore, the scanning and responding capabilities of the environment component are important assets. The ability to scan and detect environmental signals coming from environmental targets, the ability to respond swiftly to such signals, and the ability to influence the environmental targets, are significant features of this component. This environment-dependent component is highly important to competitive intelligence activities in most businesses.

4.7. Connectivity and Artificial Networks

As mentioned, quality connectivity is a key factor for successful evolution. The connectivity of the physical structure is also an important area of concern. The networks, and the integration of systems, in particular, the intelligent information systems network and the economic production system, are important components of the physical structure.

In many human organizations, a sizable component of the physical structure comprises integrated information system networks. Intelligent information system networks enhance the connectivity of the organization through better communication and faster processing of information. This feature is particularly significant in a knowledge-intensive environment. In this respect, artificial intelligent information networks partially serve as the nervous system of an intelligent organization. Highly intelligent, artificially created information systems then serve as artificial information processing nodes in intelligent organizations (see Fig. 4.6).

The central node of an information systems network includes the set of human minds, the natural thinking systems, which provide the decision-making and leadership roles of the organization. This set of natural thinking systems is the major component of the intense source. A well-connected and coherent intense source forms the center from which the orgmind emerges. It is linked to

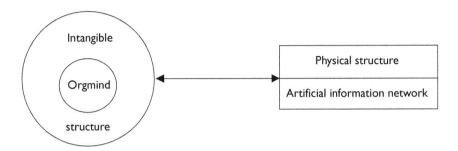

Fig. 4.6. An effective physical structure should emerge from the intangible structure and it should be supported by an artificial information network.

all other parts of the organization by the intelligent web. Within the web, there are other decision-making nodes that may possess specialization capabilities, some of which are artificial nodes.

At the moment, there are several categories of intelligent information systems that are being used in businesses. Complexity-based systems, artificial neural networks, expert systems, fuzzy logic systems, intelligent hybrid systems and knowledge management systems are some examples. However, in most organizations, these systems, if they exist, are not well integrated into a central nervous system. A highly intelligent being must possess well-integrated information processing networks and not patches of nerves here and there. An increasingly important component of the nervous system is the e-landscape. The artificial networks will be dealt with again in Chapter 7.

4.8. Conclusion

Once again the synopsis of the basic briefs and approach of the intelligent organization theory that have been discussed is captured below as the conclusion to the chapter. It is envisaged that the following suppositions are vital to the success of implementing the intelligence paradigm:

a. A structure designed around intelligence is the best option to create a smart evolver.

b. The intelligence-based approach optimizes the ability and capacity of the surface structure by improving the connectivity of the intangible structure. A well-connected intangible deep structure supports a more effective surface structure. It is important to note that the effectiveness of organizations is bounded by their overall structure.

c. An intelligence-based design helps to humanize organizations and to elevate collective intelligence.

d. An intelligence-based design places more attention on the spaces of complexity and therefore encourages more innovation and creativity.

e. An intelligence-based design stimulates self-organization. Self-organization, connectivity, emergence, evolution and collective intelligence are closely associated attributes.

f. An intelligence-based design supports co-evolution with the composite system. This dynamic creates a more sustainable intelligence advantage.

Based on the above beliefs, the first set of responsibilities to be fulfilled when adopting the intelligence strategy includes the following areas:

a. Building the orgmind and elevating collective intelligence.

b. Optimizing the contributions of the intrinsic intelligence sources.

c. Nurturing a mindset that is highly adaptive and evolving.

d. Ensuring a high level of orgmindfulness.

e. Ensuring a high level of connectivity.

f. Continuously and conscientiously tapping into latent intelligence.

g. Investing sufficient resources in the spaces of complexity.

h. Creating an intense intelligence node.

i. Creating an effective intelligence web.

j. Building an intelligent environment scanning and responding component.

k. Ensuring that the intelligent information systems network and the economic production system are synchronized (for business organizations).

   This set of pre-requisites is vital to putting an intelligent human organization in place. They form the primary initiators that can effectively make an organization more intelligent.

   In addition, the concept for organizing around intelligence encompasses three other associated perspectives. The next perspective involves organizing around knowledge and information-related activities. Natural organisms are inherently structured in this manner. The information-related activities are responsible for the information processing, knowledge structuring, thinking and decision-making capabilities of intelligent natural systems. These activities engulf the following functions:

a. Scanning the environment for relevant external information.

b. Creating useful internal information from thought processes.

c. Distributing information to all parts of the system.

d. Consuming information to update the knowledge structures.

e. Consuming information to improve decision making.

f. Creating new knowledge structures.

g. Advancing to a higher stage of discernment and existence by means of an enhanced language.

The third perspective of the intelligent organization theory involves organizing around evolution (learning, adaptation, emergence). Successful evolution means that the organism continuously adapts itself to the changing environment so that it remains alive. A living system continuously consumes information and attempts to evolve successfully. The ability to perform this function prolongs the existence of that system. Thus, human organizations must also internalize the following abilities:

a. Organizations must learn, adapt, evolve, compete and survive.

b. Organizations must learn faster than their competitors.

c. Organizations must continuously restructure through emergence and dissipation, that is, organizations must restructure to a higher order of existence by releasing the extra entropy.

d. Organizations must continuously enhance their connectivity and consequently their ability to manage evolution will be improved.

e. Organizations must maintain a high level of orgmindfulness and nurture a supportive culture to drive all the above factors.

The final perspective involves the use of complexity properties such as the butterfly effect, the rugged landscape concept and the red queen race where appropriate. These are natural nonlinear phenomena that have stimulated and sustained the existence of different forms of life and their environment. In this respect, these are also the niches that can be exploited by intelligent human organizations if the latter wish to reap the astronomical returns of nonlinearity. Intelligent organizations must be aware and ready to exploit these opportunities.

Without language our mental capacities would be poor indeed, comparable to those of the higher animals; we have, therefore, to admit that we owe our principal advantage over the beasts to the fact of living in human society.

Albert Einstein, Ideas and Opinions

V
The Human Thinking System

This chapter focuses on the macroscopic perspective of the human thinking system. The procedure in which a human mind handles one or more physical symbol systems is discussed. The conceptual development encompasses the transformation of data, information, knowledge and wisdom, and how a language emerges. The boundary of a human thinking system, the energy and matter subsystems involved, and the necessity of artificial information systems, are included.

5.1. Introduction

The human mind in which a human thinking system resides ranks among the most exciting research domains of the entire last century and it will continue to attract the same level of interest over the next few decades. It has been mentioned that "the nature of the mind...how a biological organ like the human brain can be an organ of thought...how biological organs like neurons which carry on chemical and electrical processes can support our thinking... and the processes of thinking at the level of symbols—the kind of symbolic processes that are going on when a human being thinks" are some aspects of this fascinating discipline that have captivated both information scientists and neuroscientists alike (Simon, 1989: p. 1). This group must be extended to include all individuals that manage human organizations.

At the moment, the microscopic principles and dynamics of the human brain at the neural or atomic level are still far from being fully understood. However, since Cajal confirmed that the brain is made up of a large number of discrete units using Golgi's method of staining neurons with silver salts about a hundred years ago, the neuron doctrine has been further examined by numerous researchers rigorously. Today, the brain is known to contain between 10 billion and a trillion neurons connected by about 100 trillion synapses, forming an extremely complex three-dimensional maze. The neural codes travel as electrical (energy) codes in the axon and biochemical (matter) codes in the neurotransmission. Overall, the brain generates a global neuronal pattern based on interactions at the level of the synapse.

The mechanism at the neural level that enables the brain to generate neuronal patterns remains a mystery in neuroscience. However, the discovery of the first neurotransmitter in 1973 was a significant advancement. It signified that neural codes are decipherable at the atomic level. Neuroscientists estimated that there are as many as three hundred neurotransmitters. Although this number is large, the existence of order that holds the key to unfolding the neural code must be present.

The operation of the abstract mind is equally mysterious. The cognitive or neuropsychological dimension of the mind will always remain a significant component of human behavioral analysis even after the neural mechanism of the brain is fully established. In fact, determining the relationships between the neural activities of the brain and the behavioral functions of the mind is a current key research domain. Perhaps a better understanding could be obtained using some fundamental principles from the science of complexity.

5.2. The Information-Processing Perspective

Cognitive science has always emphasized that human beings are information processors. And information processing appears to be an important connection between the function of a human thinking system and its behavior. Basically, cognitive science perceives a human thinking system as having components such as sensory memory, short-term memory, and long-term memory. Such a setup is an information-processing-related structure with capabilities to explain operations of different complexities including information processing, information consumption, concept-attainment, reasoning and decision making.

The above basis is further supported by the belief that our conscious conception of self is largely derived from our ability to acquire and use at least one natural language or a symbol system. The creation of an artificial physical symbol subsystem by the human mind leads to the extension of the natural system. The evolutionary development of the symbol subsystem is a fairly recent phenomenon in the context of evolution theory. The creation of logograms by the Sumerians took place around 3000 B.C. By 800 B.C. a complete alphabet system was finally used by the Greeks. The evolution of the above developments has altered human-thinking capabilities significantly.

Similarly, the substantive claim by neuroscience that the human brain is an information-processing machine is another strong impetus for this analysis. Almost every major development in neuroscience from the 1960s to the present has served to reinforce this claim. The assumption now is that the brain and hence human thinking systems, from both the neural and cognitive perspectives, are at least information processing systems. The convergence of all brain-mind-related studies towards information-processing activities indicates the necessity of establishing the general information theory.

Conceptualizing the general information theory is a challenging task. Since a human thinking system encompasses both a natural component as well as an artificial component, among other things, the theory must be able to account for the interactions between the artificial and the natural. The interactions include transformations of human-created entities into naturally occurring entities and vice versa. Therefore, the general information theory to be introduced must engulf a theory of artifacts that is immersed in a theory of energy and matter.

A human thinking system is an open system that interacts with its environment via a physical symbol subsystem. Therefore, it has physical symbol creation, manipulation and processing capabilities. It must also be able to convert physical symbols into information-coded energy quanta and vice versa. Subsequently, the energy quanta interact with the information-coded matter structure. Thus, it may be appropriate to define a human thinking system with respect to the knowledge already conceptualized as follows:

Definition I
A human thinking system encompasses at least an energy-matter subsystem and a physical symbol subsystem. The former is the natural component that resides in the brain while the latter is a human-created component that is an extension created by the human mind. The functional capabilities of the human thinking systems include a physical symbol perspective, a cognition perspective, an energy-matter perspective, and an underlying subatomic dimension.

With respect to the above definition, the human mind is also given a definition that reflects its boundaries and capabilities:

Definition II

The human mind is an abstract space projected by the brain's activities. It is a complex adaptive system sustained by the neural and underlying subatomic functions of the brain matter, as well as the symbol manipulation activities of the self-created physical symbol component. The boundaries of the space evolve gradually with time.

Matter that is coded with information, for example, DNA and brain matter, exhibits certain levels of intelligence capability. Very likely, a higher level of intelligence emerges when information-coded energy quanta interact with information-coded matter packages, and when the latter interact among each other. These unique activities occur only in an appropriate decoder. In this respect, there is a correlation between the level of intelligence, and the quantity and density of such matter present. The level of intelligence in turn determines the complexity of the information processing ability of such systems. Thus, intelligence and information processing abilities appear to be very closely coupled and mutually enhancing.

Natural information existing in energy-matter form is an extremely powerful latent force that determines how nature evolves and how the entire universe behaves. Thus, the universe is not dumb. It has intelligent matter that carries its "secret" codes. On the other hand, the information that exists in physical symbol form is usually created by human beings. This form of information not only enables human beings to interact with each other more meaningfully, but also enables them to understand nature in a totally different dimension, a new dimension which other living organisms have never experienced.

It may be important to mention again the existence of the intelligence spectrum and to note the difference between proto-intelligence and true intelligence. Examples of proto-intelligence are structures embedded in crystals. These are non-living systems carrying coded information. On the other hand, the latter class of systems exhibits the capacity to learn and adapt. These are higher levels intelligent systems that can manipulate symbols and possess a core structure known as the mind.

An intelligent matter system with encoded information responds to the environment. It may have complex internal activities including duplicating (reproduction) capability. The human thinking systems are prominent examples of such intelligent matter systems. The global characteristic of the human thinking systems is captured in the following general interaction equation:

$$\text{environment} \leftrightarrow \text{artifact} \leftrightarrow \text{energy} \leftrightarrow \text{matter.} \qquad (5.1)$$

This equation provides an overview of the phenomena occurring in the human mind. It also indicates that such a system has a natural component and a human-created component, and that it is an open system.

The boundaries of the physical symbol subsystem are defined by the entities of the human-created basic physical entity set, namely, data, information, knowledge and wisdom. These sets of entities are externalized entities, and each of them can be a set. In addition, the boundaries of the energy-matter subsystem are defined by the natural basic entity set, containing a set of information-coded energy quanta, and a set of neural matter packages that collectively form the information-coded matter structure. Therefore, the human-created basic physical entity set and the natural basic entity set define the operational boundaries of the human thinking systems.

Besides the natural and artificial entities, another important aspect of the human thinking systems is the intelligence space. The human thinking systems include a fairly advanced intelligence space that can be divided into four sets of functions. The first set enables the physical symbol subsystem to evolve and interact with the environment. It includes capabilities such as primitive character set creation and event capturing. The second set of functions facilitates basic entity and basic entity interactions. Therefore it includes activities such as basic entity transformation and manipulation, that is, data processing, information processing and knowledge accumulation.

The next set of functions connects the physical symbol subsystem and the energy-matter subsystem. It transforms a human-created entity into an information-coded energy quantum and vice versa, which includes the perception or concept-attainment capability. Finally, the last set of functions facilitates energy–matter and matter–matter interactions. The cognitive interpretation of such interactions includes reasoning and decision making. The neural equivalences are the information-coded energy quanta manifested as electrical signals and the information-embedded matter packages transmitted as chemical signals. The two subsystems of the human thinking system is illustrated in Fig. 5.1.

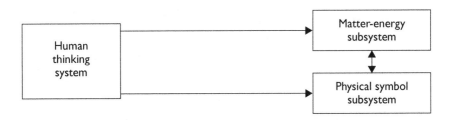

Fig. 5.1. The two subsystems of the human thinking system.

5.3. Physical Symbol Subsystem

5.3.1. *Basic intelligence and the character set*

Symbols lie at the root of intelligent action, and the symbols can be physical or nonphysical. A requirement of intelligence, at a basic level, is that such a system must have the ability to store and manipulate symbols. The characteristics of the physical symbol subsystem are defined by the equation:

$$\text{environment} \leftrightarrow \text{artifact}, \tag{5.2}$$

or

$$\text{environment} \leftrightarrow \text{basic entity}, \tag{5.3}$$

which is fundamentally a data creation and capturing phenomenon, and the equation:

$$\text{artifact} \leftrightarrow \text{artifact}, \tag{5.4}$$

or

$$\text{basic entity} \leftrightarrow \text{basic entity}, \tag{5.5}$$

which embodies the information processing and knowledge structuring processes.

The creation of a symbol set by a certain community of human beings constitutes the birth of basic (human) intelligence. It may not be too extreme to equate the above emergence to the beginning of human civilization. The discovery of this ability also distinguishes basic (human) intelligent action itself from instinctive (animal) action. This unique human trait separates humankind from the other species.

The creation of a symbol set by a particular human civilization is a fascinating phenomenon. It marks the crossing of an "intelligence threshold". The character set containing primitive elements is created by the interactions between the thinking systems and their

Fig. 5.2. The entities emerging from a physical symbol system.

environment. This event is extremely significant for all human thinking systems as its discovery signifies the extension of the natural component of the thinking system to include an artificial component, the physical symbol subsystem. The artificial component in turn facilitates the evolution of the natural component to achieve a more sophisticated level of thinking activity. This evolution has been slow, gradual and ongoing for the past few thousand years. The character set also enabled a community to store knowledge externally in written form for the first time (see Fig. 5.2).

The creation of a symbol set is only made possible by the emergence of a function to create it. Thus, there exists a symbol creation function that can create a primitive symbol or character set when a human thinking system interacts with its environment. The character set contains all the symbols that are created for the use of a particular community. In a community that uses the English language, the character set can be represented as follows:

$$C = \{a, b, c, ..., 1, 2, 3, ..., +, -, ...\}. \tag{5.6}$$

5.3.2. *Basic entity capturing and processing*

The creation of a character set leads to the emergence of a written language that facilitates event capturing and basic entity processing.

The occurrence of this event is incremental and it is made possible by the existence of certain conditions:

Axiom I

There exists at least one natural language that is not a null set and it has a character set with a large number of primitive elements.

Axiom II

There exists a coding function that can code an event into a data element or data set.

Axiom III

There exist higher-order basic entity transformation functions that transform the basic entities for better problem solving and decision making.

When an event occurs, the coding function is activated and captures the occurence of an event using the character set. The data set created contains the raw facts of the event. The coding process must observe a set of grammatical, semantic and computational rules.

Very often, additional transformations are required before the basic entity is useful. Thus, the data set has to be processed to generate a useful information set relevant to a particular situation. The information is matched against a knowledge structure. The knowledge accumulation process is perceived as a large-scale selective combination or union of related pieces of information. A knowledge structure contains chunks of information with established relationships.

5.4. The Cognitive Perspective

The psychological and neuropsychological characteristics of a human thinking system observed at the macroscopic level form the cognitive dimension. The cognitive phenomena associated with information processing and consciousness are studied at the brain code level in neuropsychology. It is at this level that a relationship between human thinking and behavior can be established.

From this perspective, perception signals are interpreted as concepts. A concept is a basic cognitive entity of the mind. And concepts interact with the cognitive structure during thinking processes. A concept is a basic cognitive entity of a human thinking system and it contains one or more pieces of related information that have been understood.

Therefore, a concept is formed when a piece or a body of information is understood. At the least, its structure and content must have been recognized. The requirement is that a concept must be meaningful, and that it can be integrated into the cognitive structure. The level of sophistication of the concept-attainment process is determined by the cognitive intelligence present. The cognitive intelligence of the human thinking systems is more complex than basic intelligence. This higher form of intelligence is denoted as advanced (human) intelligence in this model.

5.5. Advanced Intelligence

The advanced intelligence of the human mind is expressed differently from basic intelligence. It is manifested in the concept-attainment dimension. Its presence is manifested as a perception function and a decision-making function. The combinations of these two functions form a reasoning process. The existence of the two functions is vital to the evolution of advanced intelligence:

Axiom IV

There exists a perception function that maps related, human-created basic entities into a concept or a set of concepts.

Axiom V

There exists a decision function that acts on concepts or perception signals to create a decision choice and an action.

In this respect, a concept is a perception signal capturing an information state. The signal can be absorbed into the cognitive structure if it is consumed. The ability of a thinking system to handle and consume concepts indicates the presence of an advanced intelligence source.

A cognitive structure processes an intelligence source embedded within it. It is important to distinguish between the two components of a cognitive structure: the basic store of internalized information, and intelligence as the means for its internal processing. In this model, the basic store of internalized information is the cognitive space and the intelligence is the set of cognitive functions.

Information and the other basic entities are external entities with respect to the cognitive structure. A piece of information can be scanned by the mind but it is only integrated into the structure after it has been consumed or internalized, that is, after a relationship with a particular knowledge space is established. In this sense, a knowledge space is internalized within the cognitive structure while a knowledge entity is an external entity. As a particular knowledge space grows, the cognitive structure as a whole is enhanced.

Thus, there exists an internalization or consumption function that enables concepts to be integrated into the cognitive structure. The internalization function enables a concept to be consumed by the cognitive structure once the relationship between the concept and an internalized knowledge space is established. The various functions are summarized in Figs. 5.3 and 5.4.

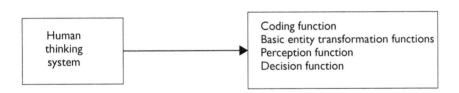

Fig. 5.3. Intelligence functions of the human thinking system.

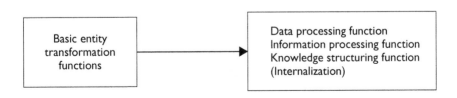

Fig. 5.4. Sub-functions of basic entity transformation.

5.6. Internalization

At this juncture, a human thinking system is perceived to have a cognitive structure comprising a cognitive space and a set of cognitive functions. The cognitive space is a store containing the various internalized knowledge spaces/structures. The union between the various knowledge spaces forms the cognitive space, and each knowledge space is therefore a subset of the cognitive space.

Internalization occurs when a concept or a set of concepts is consumed and absorbed into the cognitive space. When a concept is absorbed into a particular knowledge space, some restructuring of that space takes place. Therefore, understanding a concept, establishing the relationship between the concept and the knowledge space concerned, and finally identifying a proper fit between the two units, lead to the internalization of the concept. Thus, absorption and restructuring are necessary conditions for internalization to occur. In this regard, an internalized knowledge space can be perceived as a large collection of concepts arranged in a certain meaningful structure (see Fig. 5.5).

5.7. Energy-Matter Subsystem

5.7.1. Basic entity-energy quantum interaction

The energy-matter subsystem resides within the human brain. The general characteristics of this subsystem are captured by the two

Fig. 5.5. Internalization/consumption of a piece of information/concept.

equations:

$$\text{basic entity} \leftrightarrow \text{energy},\qquad (5.7)$$

and

$$\text{energy} \leftrightarrow \text{matter},\qquad (5.8)$$

which have been given a cognitive description earlier. It is important to analyze the brain's operations on the energy-matter basis which in turn will support the understanding of the microscopic neural dimension better.

In the energy-matter perspective, a concept is perceived as an information-coded energy quantum, and the cognitive structure is the information-embedded matter structure of the natural system. Establishing this relationship enables the role of the energy-matter subsystem to be analyzed with respect to the entire human thinking system in the energy-matter dimension.

When one or more pieces of information are assimilated by the natural component of a human thinking system, this is done by the perception function. Therefore, the perception function is also the artifact-energy conversion function, which transforms one or more pieces of information into one or more packages of information-coded energy quanta.

As an energy quantum in which information codes are embedded is a concept, the latter can be redefined in the new context as one or more related information-coded energy quanta. Similarly, the artifact-energy conversion function or perception function must also be given an energy-matter perspective. Thus, a perception function is one that has the ability to convert one or more human-created basic entities into an information-coded energy quantum.

5.7.2. *Energy quantum-matter structure interaction: Internalization*

The information-coded energy quanta created during the interaction of the two subsystems are scanned with respect to an appropriate matter knowledge structure. No consumption occurs if an energy quantum is merely scanned and rejected. Consumption of an energy quantum only happens if that quantum causes a re-organization in the matter structure. In such a case, internalization is said to have occurred. Therefore, the internalization function is an energy-matter interaction function that facilitates the knowledge restructuring process.

The matter structure is perceived as a discrete structure comprising a large number of information coded matter packages and processors (neurons). Human intelligence appears to emerge from this structure. A different perception of the internalization function must now be re-established. It is perceived as the function that enables an energy quantum to be consumed by the matter structure and in the process enhances the structure itself.

5.7.3. *Matter structure-energy quantum interaction: Externalization*

There also exists a function that enables the information-coded matter to create and emit energy quanta. This function is represented as an externalization function that acts on the matter package involved in the emission process. In the event, the matter structure creates an energy quantum when responding to the consumption of another energy quantum. Thus, there exists an externalization function that enables the matter structure to create and emit one or more energy quanta when the latter consumes an energy quantum.

It must be noted that the internalization and externalization functions are not mathematically inverse functions. Besides, the matter structure remains intact or unaltered after externalization.

The process appears to be more a duplication function where the information quantum created is identical to the portion of the matter structure concerned. Externalization is important as it enables the internal content of a thinking system to be made known to the environment.

5.7.4. *Energy quantum-basic entity interaction*

After externalization, the energy quanta created interact with the physical symbol subsystem. The energy quanta are converted into combinations of physical symbols for communication or other external manipulations. This process is executed by the energy-to-artifact conversion function. Its operation is the reverse of the perception function. Thus, there exists an energy-to-artifact conversion function that enables an information-coded energy quantum to be converted into one or more human-created basic entities. Again, the two functions may not be exact inverse functions.

5.7.5. *Matter-matter interaction*

As mentioned earlier, the matter structure is a discrete structure containing an infinitely large number of information-coded matter packages and processors. The different information-coded matter packages and processors interact among themselves internally within the structure. This activity is matter-matter interaction. It is facilitated by an intermediary matter package, a neurotransmitter. The process also leads to re-organization and enhancement of the matter structure as a whole.

Therefore, there exists a matter-matter interaction function, which can enhance the matter structure. Such interaction occurs when reasoning and decision-making processes take place in the human mind. Thus, there also exists a matter interaction function that enables information coded matter packages to interact among themselves and in the event enhances the matter structure. In this respect, matter-matter interaction and mindfulness may have an interesting relationship.

5.7.6. *Wisdom creation*

Wisdom creation is a special form of energy-matter and matter-matter interactions. It is perceived as the creation of matter packages with a new set of information codes. It is an intense self-enhancement process that is taking place within the matter structure. It is an internal process and usually it can be activated only if that particular human thinking system has been consistently consuming energy quanta in a certain knowledge domain or related areas. Very often, rigorous analysis and restructuring of the matter structure must also have taken place.

The creation of a new information state can only emerge in a mind that has made preparation for it. A reasonable knowledge space must have evolved before wisdom creation can occur. Even though wisdom has been defined as a body of new information, very often, it also encompasses the ability to conceive the new information. The consequence may amount to a discovery, an invention, or an innovative and creative contribution. Thus, the creation of wisdom is highly nonlinear. It is not merely a linear extension of the existing knowledge matter structure. Thus, this function is closely associated with complexity and nonlinearity (see Fig. 5.6).

5.7.7. *Energy-matter function space*

The energy-matter function space is an abstract space that stores the intelligence of the human thinking systems. The intelligence space is located within the discrete neuronal structure of the energy-matter subsystem. It is the dynamo of the human mind. The intelligence space is perceived to give rise to all the mental functions discussed earlier in the chapter. When activated, the intelligence

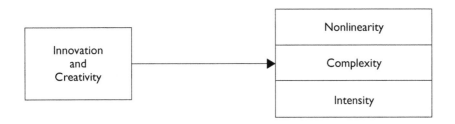

Fig. 5.6. Some characteristics of innovation and creativity.

generation function generates packages of intelligence (energy) during neuronal activities. In this respect, intelligence is quantized and very likely, consciousness is also quantized. It is the large quantity of intelligence packages emitted at one point in time that makes intelligence appear to be a continuum. Thus, there exists an intelligence function that manipulates the intelligence space.

In this respect, a human thinking system is a concentrated source of intelligence. It is probably the most intense source of intelligence on earth. However, the universe as a whole embodies infinite sources of intelligence, in particular, at the proto-intelligence level. In general, all intelligent systems, natural and artificial, living and non-living, contain some degree of structured information. In this sense, intelligence is the ability or power to decode and process data embedded in the universe. It is a mysterious energy created by nature to decode itself. The degree of decoding depends on the intelligence of the decoder.

5.8. Conclusion

At the moment, the above conceptualization only provides a fundamental structure that can explain the macroscopic dynamics of the human thinking systems. The theory perceives human thinking systems as intelligent open systems that interact with their immediate environment. Such systems have a natural component and a human-created component that substantially enhance their capabilities of the former.

Besides the macroscopic dynamics, human thinking systems also have a neuronal and subatomic dimension as well as a complex adaptive perspective. The general information theory conceived to explain the human mind must take care of all these perspectives. When that is achieved, the mysterious phenomena that enable the material brain to give rise to a non-material abstract mind with a behaviorial dimension will be fully understood.

At this juncture, it may be appropriate to conclude this chapter on the human thinking system by putting in place the postulates of the general information theory:

Postulate I: Law of Boundary
Data, information, knowledge, and wisdom are the human-created basic entities, and information-coded energy quanta as well as information-coded matter packages are the natural entities that define the boundaries of the general information theory.

Postulate II: First Law of Interaction
The basic objective of all human-created entity interaction is to transform a physical entity with higher entropy to one with lower entropy so that the concept-attainment and decision-making processes can be enhanced.

Postulate III: Second Law of Interaction
The basic objective of energy–matter and matter–matter interaction is to enhance the matter knowledge structure of a human thinking system so that it can function more effectively. In this respect, both the information-coded matter subspace and the intelligence subspace are enriched by the above interaction.

Postulate IV: Law of Artificial Systems
The primary objectives of all constructed basic entity systems (including the computerized information systems) are to achieve the first law of interaction more effectively using artificial means, and to support the second law of interaction by complementing the shortcomings of the natural component of a human thinking system.

With a better comprehension of the human mind on a macroscopic perspective, the more complex aspect of the interactive dynamics of human organization, encompassing autopoiesis, self-organization, evolution and co-evolution, as well as the interdependency of characteristics/properties of complex adaptive systems will be examined over the next few chapters.

Mindfulness is considered as the strongest strand, for it plays an important role in the acquisition of both calm and insight. Mindfulness is awareness (of the mind); it is a certain function of the mind and, therefore, is a mental factor. Without this all-important factor of mindfulness one cannot cognize sense objects, one cannot be fully aware of one's behavior.

Piyadassi Thera, The Buddha's Ancient Path

VI
Basic Intelligence Dynamic and the Intelligent Person Model

In this chapter, the evolution and co-evolution dynamics of ecosystems are examined and compared to the processes of human organizations more explicitly. A special focus on businesses as complex adaptive systems is included. The individual local self-centric and the global org-centric evolutionary dynamics of intelligent organizations and their interacting agents are investigated. The intelligent person model is introduced. How the intelligent person as a smarter evolver helps to bind a group of human thinking systems and elevate the collective intelligence of the organization through mindfulness, orgmindfulness and co-evolution is also conceived. (For better connectivity, some concepts discussed earlier are further reinforced in this chapter.)

6.1. Introduction

The Darwinian theory suggests that evolution is a gradual process, adopting a tactician approach. The process is a survival of the fittest. A subsequent discovery indicates that this claim of Darwin and Wallace may not have been totally right. The observation of sudden increase and the richness of life forms existing on the earth during the Cambrian era suggested that there is a contradiction. This event, termed the Cambrian explosion, took place very swiftly about

600 million years ago, after three billion years of biological silence. Thus, evolution does not appear to be entirely a gradual process.

Another important discovery is the property of spontaneous order or "order for free". This property indicates that self-organization is an intrinsic characteristic of complex genetic systems, and probably of all complex adaptive systems. Basically, there is no need for any external forces to execute or influence an evolution process. Self-organization emerges when the system reaches certain level of criticality. In this respect, it is an intrinsic activity of nature due to internal forces existing within the systems. These latent internalized forces are the impetus from the dynamo behind structure, life and human organizations. And they are manifested as intelligence.

As stipulated earlier, the second law of thermodynamics states that the universe is expanding, entropy is increasing, and the phenomenon itself is chaotic. However, in the sea of chaos there are countless "local activity centers", each surrounded by a space of order that defies the second law. In each of these spaces, a structure emerges, entropy is reduced, and predictability is enhanced. The space of order is the space of established structure where predictability is high, if not absolutely accurate. These local activity centers include a crystal, an amoeba, the human thinking system, and even a community of human beings.

The linear world that humankind is familiar with will continue to exist and serve as the comfortable primordial stratum. However, the more embracing and unexplored frontiers of the nonlinear domain should be the next territory to be exploited if human beings are to progress further into the intelligence era. As niches and focus areas have changed, understanding and exploiting the fundamental characteristics of complexity and nonlinearity is crucial. Similarly, businesses whose functions encompass nonlinear activities such as strategic planning, creating competitive advantage, and structuring organization must also exploit complexity in the new context.

6.2. Complex Adaptive Features and Human Structure

It is now understood that the human thinking systems as well as all human organizations are complex, adaptive and nonlinear. The first distinction is the presence of great diversification in surface phenomena arising from a fairly simple set of elementary processes, due to only slight variations in initial conditions, the butterfly effect. The set of elementary processes operating in every brain must be similar, however, the macroscopic characteristics, the behavior of individuals is vastly different. The complex behaviorial patterns versus the same set of simple elementary processes, makes the brain and hence the mind, a complex adaptive system. Thus, the proliferation of behaviorial patterns due to small variations in initial conditions is a significant property to note. The implication is that a person's behavior can be greatly altered by just small changes in conditions.

Another vital characteristic of such systems is their ability to encrypt information about themselves and their environment. A piece of snowflake contains information. The genetic message of human beings is encoded in DNA. In today's societies, the human brains carry highly sophisticated and complex knowledge structures. Similarly, intelligent human organizations must also possess the equivalent genetic packages, the organizational (societal) DNA. Identifying and strengthening organizational DNA is a new responsibility of community, business and political leaders.

The encoded information in any structure can only be decoded when intelligence is present. Intelligence is associated with a spectrum of information-related activities. At the higher end of the spectrum, intelligence energy tends to create more distinct order through self-centric/autopoietic or self-enrichment processes with respect to a certain local order center. This reinforcement of local structure is a basic characteristic of life. Thus, order and structure are created against the expanding universe and increasing entropy. When this activity reaches a certain level of sophistication, consciousness emerges inherently.

In this respect, all complex adaptive systems that evolve successfully with time have to be innovative and creative to a great extent. They shift or transform from one state to another state, responding to changes in conditions of the system and its environment. There actually exists certain preferred states or attractors that the system will move into swiftly, depending on the overall conditions. This observation noted in complexity theory has significant implications on organization strategy because an intelligence advantage can be created if a preferred state is quickly recognized and adopted/exploited.

Potentially, the first mover advantage is highly critical. At a punctuation point or phase transition great changes take place quickly. A slight change in conditions can lead to a huge transformation, for instance, when water solidifies into a cube of ice, and when unicellular organisms become multi-cellular organisms such as during the Cambrian era. Thus, at these points, complex adaptive systems move very swiftly into a new state, similar to a revolution or a discovery. Subsequently, the changes that take place become slower again. The various characteristics that can be manifested by intelligent human organizations are captured in Fig. 6.1.

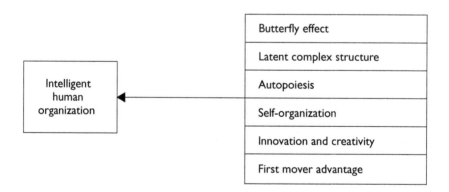

Fig. 6.1. Some complex adaptive features that are beneficial to human organizations if exploited correctly.

6.3. Intelligence Decoder

The universe is coded with information, ranging from crystal, DNA, human brain, human organization, nation, and eventually to a global society. All these examples are systems embedded with varying forms of structure. Information is the capacity to organize and structure systems, and organized systems contain information. This bilateral relationship is fascinating and vital to the emergence of life. However, as indicated earlier, the embedded information by itself may not be very meaningful. It must be decoded with respect to a certain environmental context.

The existence of an appropriate decoder is essential for the encoded information in energy and matter forms to be understood, released and utilized (see Fig. 6.2). In the microbiological world, a cell decodes the information stored in a DNA. In the socio-economical and political dimensions, the human minds are the key information decoders. Hence, with the new understanding, the human minds must be the fundamental focal points in all human organizations. Their functions, as well as the means to improve their performance at individual, team and organizational levels must be allocated high priority and better understood. Basically, the human thinking systems must be made to function as better information decoders.

Therefore, intelligence and information are two closely associated entities with mutually reinforcing relationships. Intelligence is the unique intangible energy that drives all human thinking systems.

Fig. 6.2 Function of an intelligence decoder.

The more sophisticated the information processing capability, the higher the level of intelligence. Intelligence is spread over a spectrum, with the collective intelligence of a global nation being the optimal on this planet.

6.4. Management of Human Organizations

6.4.1. *Organization theory*

Human beings have come together to form groups as early as they were cave dwellers. Since the industrial revolution, the intention and characteristics of some human organizations have changed drastically. The historical development of organization theory has been stimulating, as several schools of thoughts have emerged during the last century. The contributions of management organization theorists embrace numerous domains such as executive leadership, management function, management strategy, operational procedure, organization objective and productivity.

In the new context, some old concepts may remain intact. For instance, Davis suggested that the primary objective of a business organization is economic service and the creation of products and/or services to generate economic utilities so that the organization can survive is still true to a large extent. Similarly, the elements of management such as planning, organizing, command, co-ordination and control may remain a significant requisite set. However, some of these elements may have to be more closely scrutinized. They have to be executed with greater subtlety. In addition, new elements may have to be added as old ones are redefined.

Leadership is another vital attribute that requires re-examination. It links organizational objectives, business functions, destinations and other economic activities together. Davis stated that management is the function of executive leadership. Its purpose is to determine an effective economical basis for the accomplishment of designated objectives. In this respect, economic leadership may still be a crucial component of management. Although, a school of thought believes that leadership and management are two totally different qualities. Whatever the current belief is, leadership in general may have to be revolutionalized and collective leadership may emerge.

At the moment, business functions are broadly classified as managerial and operative. The operative functions appear to be more structured relative to the managerial functions. The most significant contributions to the operative aspect of management have been attributed to Taylor. In the most structured form, a unit of operative function is a single, simple act of operative performance, either mental or physical. It has definite starting and ending points. This concept is fundamental to the techniques of time and motion study.

The managerial aspect of business function is more complex, as it includes the more sophisticated problem solving and decision-making perspective. This association articulates that the decision-making model of Simon, and the bounded rationality concept of March and Simon, are important reference sources. In the current context, all the human thinking systems, assisted by artificially constructed information systems are responsible for executing the business function set that an organization possesses. As decision-making processes take place in the human mind, the intelligence sources are becoming even more important in the new form of organization.

Thus, in human resource management, the key perspectives are no longer the same. The shift from menial/skills to intelligence/knowledge is inevitable. In this respect, the theory of organization science has to be revamped. In this chapter, the Kuhn's traditional scientific approach is adopted to examine the structured and linear aspect of the economic production subsystem of business organizations. This aspect is included to provide a more holistic explanation of businesses as complex adaptive systems. Subsequently, the complex and nonlinear domain of the human thinking systems is incorporated to illustrate that all human organizations are composite complex adaptive systems.

6.4.2. *Economic entity transformation*

To construct an organization/management theory with attributes that could accommodate the new observations/understandings stipulated in the earlier chapters, a paradigmatic shift that encompasses a scientific dimension must be established. The conceptualization of a theoretical scientific model starts with the identification of variables or constructs. The model should specify the manner in which these entities interact with each other. The boundary of the model must be determined by examining both the intrinsic and interactive properties of the entities involved. The complexity, nonlinearity and intelligence perspectives are new domains that must be explored/exploited eventually. It is the latter that is perceived as the intelligence strategic aspect of the new organization science.

Traditionally, all human organizations are always established with certain basic objectives in mind. For instance, a business organization is a set-up that pools various business functions together to generate revenue. Such a system must be an open system. It must be prepared to accept input and to deliver output. The input consists of the economic resources, and the output, products and services. The business functions are certain operative and managerial functions that enable the input to be converted into the output. Such a transformational process is guided by a primary objective. This objective is to optimize profit.

Besides, a business organization is also a looped system. This feature ensures that the transformational processes can be fine-tuned and controlled. The managerial functions play a significant role in the feedback process. Thus, in such a model, a business organization is perceived and examined as a looped open system, accepting economic resources as input and manufactured products and/or services as output. The entire mechanism is made possible by a set of business functions, including the production processes.

To ensure the continuity of this conceptualization, it will be more meaningful to begin by examining briefly the intrinsic properties of the various economic resources that are identified as the basic entities. Material and labor are the physical entities. These entities are valued for the physical state in which they exist. And they constitute direct input into organizations. On the other hand, information is a rather different type of economic entity. Even though it exists in physical form (very often in symbolic form), by itself it is useless until it is consumed to create a concept that has meaning and value (as mentioned in the previous chapter). Thus, internalization must occur if a piece of information is to be regarded as being consumed by a human thinking system. In this respect, information is a conceptual entity and it can be re-used.

Money is another entity that has a different fundamental characteristic. It is a pseudo-entity or an indirect economic entity. The money entity is used to obtain the three economic entities mentioned earlier. In this sense, if an organization has a sufficient supply of the other three entities, money becomes redundant (barter trade). Money is basically an intermediary created by human beings to store wealth more efficiently. Hence, the four input economic entities utilized are information, labor, material and money.

Correspondingly, there are two output economic entities: the product and service entities. A product is a physical economic entity while service is an intangible economic entity. The output economic entities are assumed to be more valuable compared to the input economic entities. Otherwise, the transformations used to convert them from the input to the output state are irrelevant and unnecessary. As each of these entities or entity states has a utility value associated with it, the utility value of an output state is assumed to be greater than that of an input state. This fact must be true in general. Therefore, the assumption is that there are always consumers that value the output economic entities more than the raw materials. And economic production is basically the transformation of input economic entities into output economic entities.

Business organizations are operational because of the existence of certain business functions. Such functions are assumed to exist in the mind of the staff, and are also found in the artificially constructed systems including information and production systems. Historically, five such operative and managerial functions have been recognized in business organizations and their transformational characteristics are uniquely different from one another. These functions are stated as the first five axioms of the model (see Fig. 6.3):

Axiom I
There exists a buying function that has the ability to transform a money entity input state into a primary economic entity input state.

Axiom II
There exists an operative (production) function, manual and/or automated, which transforms a primary economic entity input state into a primary economic entity output state.

Axiom III
There exists a selling function that has the ability to transform a primary economic entity output state into a money entity output state.

Axiom IV
There exists a "production/economic-oriented" managerial function that complements the production or operative function to increase the profit of the organizational systems.

Axiom V
There exists a "socio-psychologically-oriented" managerial function that minimizes the socio-psychological/stress and political disturbances in organizations.

Economic entity transformation

Fig. 6.3. The basic economic entity production cycle.

Based on the identification and discussion of the six economic entities and their properties, and the basic operations in the business function set, the first postulate of the economic entity transformation model, the law of boundaries, is stated:

Postulate I: Law of Boundaries
The scope of the spaces of order of business organizations is defined by the elements of the input economic entity states and the elements of the output economic entity states, namely information, labor, material, money, product and service, as well as the transformational characteristics of the business function set.

Concurrently, the other fundamentals of the spaces of order are summarized in the next two postulates as the law of interaction and the law of organization:

Postulate II: Law of Interaction
The primary objective of a business organization for transforming an economic entity input state into an economic entity output state is to generate profit.

Postulate III: Law of Organization
The key purpose for establishing a business organization and hence for setting up an economic entity transformation system is to optimize the law of interaction.

Apparently, besides economic production/transformation, a socio-psychological subsystem is present in all businesses. Axiom V assumes that there exists a socio-psychologically-oriented managerial function that manages this social behavioral perspective. In addition, a business organization is a combination of an economic production subsystem and a socio-psychological subsystem intertwined in a rather complex manner. This reality indicates that complexity and nonlinearity are also present in all business organizations.

A latest observation reveals that some new business organizations do not even possess the basic economic entity transformation subsystem. Many of the fastest moving businesses in the world are knowledge-intensive organizations, and their sole activity is selling the knowledge and expertise of their employees, rather than manufacturing products or providing services. This new breed of business organizations further signifies the importance of a change in mindset and further reinforces the significance of organizing around intelligence. Human beings are valued more for their thinking systems and not their labor. More and more businesses are discovering that the value of their human capital and intellectual property are exceeding their material assets. The knowledge to exploit knowledge more effectively is highly valued in the new environment.

6.4.3. *New management and leadership mindset*

Apparently, business organizations and all human organizations, similar to biological and ecological systems, possess both spaces of order and complexity. They are complex adaptive systems. However, the structure of the spaces of order of human organizations in its present form is revealing its inefficiency. The current theories and practices "based on the view of an organization as a production machine, people as the major parts of the machine, and systems as engineered linear structures" are no longer valid (McMaster, 1996: p. 6). Such theories, practices and structures created for the industrial era are misfits in the new knowledge economy.

The tremendous amount of emphasis placed on the surface structure alone, in particular the linear perspective, must be avoided. The newly discovered landscape of complexity and nonlinearity has to be allocated higher priority. Although the mechanistic, rigid and tangible structure of the spaces of order is important, the intangible and dynamical deep structure of organizations is even more crucial. In intelligent organizations, it is the complex deep structure that binds the systems and provides the basis for the surface structure to be better conceived and constructed.

In this respect, the spaces of complexity, including the individual and group thinking dynamics must be explored, understood and exploited. Even though the set of basic entities and the set of elementary processes stipulated in the economic entity transformation model will remain as the fundamental component for many business organizations, the intelligence enhancing function is swiftly assuming a more crucial role. Especially, for businesses that solely provide the expertise of their employees. As intelligence enhancing function is nonlinear in nature, it magnifies the importance of the socio-psychological subsystem and diminishes the status of the economic production subsystem. The axiom specifying the intelligence enhancing function is stipulated as follows:

Axiom VI

There exists an intelligence enhancing function that enables latent intelligence in organizations to be exploited, and collective intelligence and connectivity to be nurtured.

Thus, human organizations are able to perform more effectively only if they are able to exploit the intelligence enhancing function more optimally. A new organization form that is structured around intelligence is a new necessity. It must be emphasized again that the human thinking systems, the primary sources of intelligence in all organizations, must be allocated top priority so as to elevate both social and mental bindings. The collective intelligence of organizations can only be enhanced through the deeper interaction of the intrinsic intelligence sources. In this respect, a human organization is perceived to possess a life and exist as a unique evolutionary entity. Thus, a new niche is to structure a human organization as a community of human beings working together to survive by optimizing their intrinsic and collective intelligence. The deep/inner dynamic of such an intelligent structure is further examined below.

6.5. Intelligent Human Organization

6.5.1. Local self-enrichment processes

In any evolving systems, the smallest unit of interest, the elementary unit, is an extremely significant entity. An elementary unit is the smallest unit capable of independent existence in the system under examination. The evolutionary success or failure of these units determines the fate of the systems. Successful elementary units help to stabilize the systems and unsuccessful units propagate instability. This is analogous to atoms as the basic building blocks of elements and compounds.

In human organizations, the elementary units are human beings or more specifically, the human thinking systems. Business organizations are human systems formed with the basic objective of pooling different human abilities or expertise together to create certain synergetic effects in business/economic operations. Even with the advent and extensive application of technologies, human beings must remain the most significant entities in all human organizations, as the intrinsic intelligent sources are embedded in the human brains. Therefore, the presence and significance of intrinsic intelligence in the elementary units and collective intelligence in human systems are stated in the next two axioms:

Axiom VII
The elementary units of intelligent human organizations, the human thinking systems, are driven by their own intrinsic intelligence. Each of these units is a complex adaptive system.

Axiom VIII
All intelligent human organizations possess their own collective intelligence. Hence they are higher order/composite intelligent complex adaptive systems.

The elementary units of human systems are influenced and controlled by certain elementary forces that are self-centric or autopoietic. These primary forces controlling all human decision-making are the self-enrichment processes. Thus, the self-enrichment forces, analogous to attractive physical forces are centripetal in nature. They focus on strengthening the local structure and prolong the existence of the individual elementary entities. For instance, even in the matter world (the non-living world), atoms that are self-sufficient do not react. They are highly stable. A group of such atoms, the noble gases, is totally inert. They are fully self-sufficient. However, other atoms that are not self-sufficient will react through sharing (covalent bond) and transfering/receiving (electrovalent bond) electrons.

In the human world, the autopoietic possesses are similar, except these self-enrichment processes are not necessarily material based.

Thus, rendering the dynamic even more complex. Mental, spiritual, self-actualization and other forms of enrichment are equally significant. Although, for many people at the moment, the socio-economical dimension still appears to predominate. The existence of these elementary self-enrichment processes is stated as the next axiom of the model:

Axiom IX
There exist autopoietic elementary self-enrichment processes that constantly enhance the stability of the elementary units in all intelligent human organizations.

Thus, the elementary self-enrichment processes constitute the first set of primary stabilizing forces in human systems. Under all circumstances, these elementary processes cannot be ruthlessly suppressed or totally deactivated. In certain communist regimes, for instance, where individuals are asked to make sacrifices for the nation to the extent that their own interests are completely ignored, the expected surface phenomenon never materialize. Instead, a very different outcome emerges. In this case, the systems disintegrated. Although a fundamental belief in the communist ideology is actually to stablize the elementary units, the practice has been otherwise. Apparently, the elementary units must be stabilized first before the system in which they are elements, can ever be stabilized.

Therefore, in human organizations once the self-enrichment processes vanish, the system destabilizes and quickly disintegrates. Such a consequence is due to the fact that the most basic layer of the system is not in proper order. Complexity exceeds connectivity. The internal dynamic becomes chaotic and the expected surface phenomenon does not materialize. The adaptive system can no longer adapt or evolve. This important understanding is stated as the next postulate of the model:

Postulate IV: Law of Self-Enrichment
Self-enrichment of the elementary units is the most funda-mental requirement for the successful evolution of all human organizations. (Self-enrichment processes form the first set of primary stabilizers in such systems.)

The degree of self-enhancement needed by an elementary unit is subjective with respect to the individual units concerned. However, local optimization associated with the concept of an economic man rarely materializes. In addition, due to the constraints of the think-ing system of the elementary units, there are limits to optimizing a decision or an action. This is the administrative man concept. The bounded rationality model indicates that the inner dynamic of the individual elementary unit is very important. However, the inner dynamic of the human thinking systems is extremely complex as well. Later in this chapter, the inner dynamic of an intelligent per-son as a smart evolver will be introduced.

6.5.2. Global forces

In the atomic world, the structure of an atom must be intact before a molecule can be formed. And the purpose of forming a molecule is to further increase the stability of the respective atoms. Similarly, a piece of element or compound is created for the same reason. The atoms and molecules come together to stabilize themselves within a larger system. In the biological world, similar group instinct exists. Colonies of various kinds are common sight, and in many respects, colonies are more successful evolvers than loners. Thus, the integration of evolution and co-evolution of a system and its elementary units is a common phenomenon in nature.

In systems where human beings are the elementary units, the dynamic manifested is the same. A few human beings are attracted to form a group and to participate in the groups' activities fundamentally for better self-enrichment. The size of the group can be increased to that of a corporation, an economy, or a nation. In addition, when a group is established, global forces and self-organization emerge spontaneously as well. Self-organization has also been observed in the matter world. For instance, when the condition is right, crystallization takes place spontaneously. Again, the phenomenon occurs to strengthen both the existence of the individual atoms and the collection of atoms that now exists as a crystal.

Thus, the global forces support the survival of the systems. However, the global forces of these systems must simultaneously enhance the elementary self-enrichment processes and sustain the existence of the system if they are to be effective. The next axiom stipulates this requirement:

Axiom X
There exist global forces that further enrich the elementary units, that is, global forces must enhance the self-enrichment processes if they are to be regarded as constructive.

Apparently, the strangeness of constructive global forces is that, although they are globally focused, they interact with the local elementary self-enrichment processes to ensure that the complex dynamic system evolves and survives successfully together with its interacting agents. On the contrary, global forces that interrupt or suppress elementary self-enrichment possesses have negative contributions. Thus, the overall dynamic of human organizations is inherently an interaction between the self-enrichment processes and the constructive global forces. The entire dynamic is cyclical and emergence in nature.

Postulate V: Law of Global Forces

The effective global forces in intelligent human organizations are those that further enrich the elementary units of the systems, that is, they must enhance the elementary self-enrichment processes. Therefore, the presence of constructive global forces is essential for successful evolution of all intelligent organizations. (This set of constructive global forces forms the next set of system stabilizers.)

Therefore, the notion that global interest should be enforced and be placed above that of the elementary units at all costs does not support the expected global phenomenon. If a business organization places too much priority on its corporate interest and ignores those of its employees, the set-up will collapse eventually. When the elementary units observe that the elementary self-enrichment activities are being suppressed, the system will self-destruct. It is only through enhancing the elementary processes with constructive global forces that the expected system phenomena can emerge. Thus, the subtlety that leads to successful competition and survival of an intelligent organization in the knowledge economy lies in the state of its human thinking systems. This is a new critical success factor (see Fig. 6.4).

6.5.3. Intelligent system dynamic, mindfulness and orgmindfulness

Primarily, it must be recognized and respected that the self-enrichment dynamic of the individual human beings is a vital local

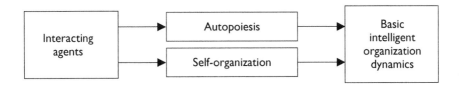

Fig. 6.4. The two complex dynamics in intelligent human organization.

self-centric phenomenon. Its basic objective is to strengthen the local structure and to prolong the existence of the individual units. This dynamic is driven by the intelligence embedded in the human thinking systems. In most circumstances, the multi-dimensional needs of human beings encompassing the material, mental and spiritual perspectives render the system dynamic of human organizations very complex.

As the self-enrichment processes emerge from the individual interacting agents, conceptually the global forces emerge concurrently from the orgmind. An organization is intelligent only if it is able to nurture a high level of collective intelligence. A dynamic equilibrium state of the system is determined by the interaction between the elementary processes and the global forces. Thus, an intelligent organization must be able to bind the individuals and the latter must be able to influence the system positively at the same time. This loop of forces enhances the elementary units and simultaneously allows the global system to learn, adapt and evolve. A human organization with intense collective intelligence self-organizes when the condition is right. As a new stable surface structure emerges, a better and more effective system is perceived to come into existence. The entire dynamic is nonlinear, complex and continuous. The focus is on both the evolution and co-evolution of the system and its elementary units.

Fig. 6.5. Mindfulness is an internally focused mental function that enhances the overall evolution dynamic.

Fig. 6.6. An orgmindful human organization always monitors the mental state of its interacting agents.

The elementary self-enrichment processes, the primary set of internalized forces that drive human organizations could be modified by a mindful mind (illustrated in Fig. 6.5). Thus, the mental state of the thinking system is a crucial factor. The mindfulness of the individual minds is a vital new attribute. Similarly, for an organization, orgmindfulness is another crucial property. An organization is orgmindful if it constantly focuses inwards to ensure that all its interacting agents are in a stable and highly participative state (see Fig. 6.6). Thus, the collective intelligence source is effective only if it is able to influence the mindfulness of the individual thinking systems. This bilateral relationship is extremely significant and delicate in intelligent organizations. It enhances connectivity and

Fig. 6.7. Orgmindfulness nurtures better connectivity and a mindful culture.

supports the emergence of a more supportive mindful culture, as illustrated in Fig. 6.7.

In this respect, the state of the orgmind is an extremely vital property in a knowledge-intensive environment. A highly coherent and dynamic intangible structure only evolves from a very well focused orgmind with intense collective intelligence. Orgmindfulness enhances the evolution and co-evolution of the system and its interacting agents. The organization becomes aware of the significance of the mental state of each and every interacting human thinking system. This important understanding is summarized as the next two postulates of the intelligent organization theory:

Postulate VI: Law of Collective Intelligence
The collective intelligence of an intelligent organization resides in its orgmind and it is a vital energy source that is responsible for moulding a coherent deep structure and an effective nimble surface structure. Without the presence of collective intelligence a human organization is retarded.

> **Postulate VII:** Law of Orgmindfulness
> A high level of orgmindfulness is necessary to nurture an intense, coherence and well focused collective intelligence source. Otherwise, the evolution and co-evolution dynamics of the organization and its interacting agents will not be effective.

6.6. Intelligent Person Model

Apparently, the human thinking system is the most important asset of a human being. This is true for all living systems in this world. Once the thinking system ceases to function, the person ceases to exist. The human mind comes into existence because of the emergence of consciousness. Otherwise, it will remain as a brain, merely a biological organ, like a kidney. In this case, there will be no difference between a biological system and an automated mechanical machine. Thus, the human mind, a unique intangible abstract space projected by the intense intelligence of the human brain is a vital entity. Even though the mind is intangible, its presence is overwhelmingly felt.

Consciousness emerges only when intelligence crosses a certain threshold. The consciousness of a human mind makes a human being aware of his/her own existence as an independent entity. Subsequently, the mental functions such as awareness, perception, reasoning and decision making arise. This state of awareness is further enhanced by the presence of the sensory system, an intelligent subsystem that provides a human being with the abilities to interact with the environment. The sensory input helps a person to act and react to the changing conditions more effectively. Most human beings today are highly aware of their environment. Consequently, autopoiesis emerges. Otherwise, once the intelligence source is eradicated, the physical system in which the mind resides will be swiftly absorbed into the chaotic main flow of the universe.

To sustain itself as a unique conscious intelligence source, a human mind has to be extremely mindful too. Mindfulness emerges only when the mind is highly conscious. It is the awareness of each and every thought that arises in the mind. It creates directed inward attention and teaches the mind to be more focused of itself. In this respect, mindfulness is different from awareness in its general usage. Mindfulness is an internal self-search mental function. It is a highly valued attribute that also enhances rationality. It is a mental function that only exists in a highly conscious mind. Mindfulness can be better achieved when the brain is in the alpha, theta and delta states, that is, when the mind is more serene and less confused. The brain waves in these states have frequency between 1 to 13 Hz. In addition, mindfulness and creativity are also intimately related. Thus, a more mindful mind is usually more innovative and creative. Very likely, this mental function of mindfulness only exists in the human mind and not in any other living species on this planet.

Right mindfulness and clear comprehension are two significant attributes that guide the inner dynamic of an intelligent person into better self-organization. It is when the mind is mindful that the other activities such as perception, problems solving and decision making are executed effectively. As an action arises from a thought, a mindful mind being more internally focused will eventually generate a more rational longer-term decision and action. Thus, in a highly intelligent mind, there exists a deeper organizing center. This center continually reminds the mind to be mindful. In an intelligent person, a very high order of mindfulness must be present at all times to sustain a high level of rationality.

In this manner, an intelligent person frequently modifies and introduces additional meanings to its self-enrichment processes. A more subtle approach is usually adopted compared to an ordinary thinking system. An intelligent person ensures that he/she has better long-term survival opportunities. The evolution of an intelligent person also encompasses co-evolution with the system, that is, there is also an orgmindfulness component. Such an intelligent person seeks holistic adaptive solutions. In this respect, an adaptive solution may not be optimum (total rationality of an economic man) or even satisficing at a particular moment in time (bounded rationality of an administrative man). Due to mental, physical and environmental constraints, the solution may even be an option with short-term losses that eventually leads to longer-term gains.

For instance, an intelligent person may not expect to put the knowledge acquired during a short training program into immediate practice. The intelligent person realizes that his/her knowledge chunks are not sufficiently large to bring about the desired change. He/she also recognizes the significant of the holistic perspective of the system, that is, there may be many other factors involved. However, if the condition is right the intelligent person will orchestrate a change, and will allow the change to emerge. An intelligent person is always aware that an effective change may not take place overnight.

Thus, being highly adaptive and nonlinear, an intelligent person focuses on longer-term survival, and also helps to create a more positive system phenomenon through the use of both deliberate and emergent strategies. In this respect, an intelligent person is always making preparation for the sudden appearance of punctuation points. In addition, as the self-organization processes of human organizations are highly dependent on the mental state of the individual interacting agents, these processes can be greatly enhanced by interacting agents that are highly intelligent. Fundamentally, if self-organization could take place in atoms with very low proto-intelligence when the condition is right, a group of highly intelligent persons with a very high level of collective intelligence should

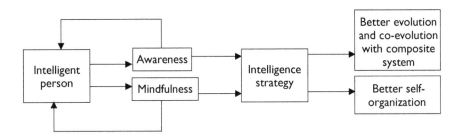

Fig. 6.8. Basic dynamic of an intelligent person as a smarter evolver.

self-organize even more effectively at criticality. This concept is illustrated in Fig. 6.8.

6.7. Conclusion

This chapter reinforces the fact that the evolution of all natural systems, including human organizations, is driven by intelligence. Intelligence is the mysterious intangible entity created by nature to drive its own evolutionary and co-evolutionary dynamics. The more advanced systems learn quickly, create sophisticated knowledge structure, and adapt to fast changing environment continuously. In addition, intelligence is not merely computational competency. Thinking, or for that matter, logical and rational thinking, is a necessary attribute that indicates the presence of advanced intelligence.

The basic dynamic of intelligent organizations has a self-centric as well as an org-centric component. The autopoietic self-enrichment processes are essential for individual survival. Coupled with the global forces of the composite system, the interacting agents co-evolve with the organization. The combined dynamic is responsible for nurturing collective intelligence, connectivity, and a supportive and mindful culture that are desperately needed in all intelligent organizations.

This observation leads to the conceptualization of the intelligent person model. An intelligent person besides being highly aware of the environment also maintains a highly mindful mind at all times. Such a mental state in an interacting agent is vital if humankind wishes to move into a more advanced state of development. In addition, an intelligent person being also orgmindful helps to expedite the nurturing of collective intelligence in an organization. Thus, an intelligent interacting agent always attempts to establish a more supportive culture in the organization through improving the quality of its connectivity, competitiveness and evolution and co-evolution dynamics. This is a cyclical process that requires the intelligent interacting agent and the system to continually identify new equilibriums, guided by the core properties of chaos theory. The learning and adjustment process between the system and the agent is continual and may have no known destination. This is also the basic mindset of an intelligent person.

Finally, some additional features to note when nurturing an intelligent organization are as follows:

a. The dynamic of an intelligent human organization is an integration of local self-enrichment processes and constructive global forces.

b. The mental state of the interacting agents as well as the orgmind has an extremely significant impact on the overall system dynamic.

c. An interacting agent that is an intelligent person ensures a more constructive system dynamic. Such a person possesses three basic characteristics, namely, a high level of mindfulness, more concern about longer-term optimality rather than shorter-term gain, and highly aware of the presence of emergence. Thus, an intelligent person is able to adapt to punctuation points better, and better self-organization will also take place spontaneously in a system of intelligent persons at criticality.

d. Therefore, the mindfulness of an interacting agent and the orgmindfulness of a human organization must be allocated high priority when leading and managing the organization. Only then can a higher level of collective intelligence and a more supportive culture be nurtured.

Technology is not the limiting factor in creating a knowledge management environment—it is the management of the technology and culture that greatly influences the success of knowledge management endeavors.

Jay Liebowitz, Building Organizational Intelligence

VII
Artificial Intelligent Information Systems Network

This chapter introduces the roles and needs of artificial information systems networks in intelligent human organizations. These networks support the efficiency of the physical structure by increasing the speed of information processing and transmission, elevating the capacity of knowledge storage, and improving the quality of connectivity and organizational learning. The common intelligent artificial information systems are briefly discussed.

7.1. Introduction

It has been noted in Chapter 1 that besides the awakening to intelligence, complexity and nonlinearity, there are two other significant changes that have also altered the environment in which business organizations operate and compete. The first change is the emergence and strengthening of a global economy. The implication of this transformation is that an organization does not only compete with its local competitors but also with those in other parts of the world. The way to evaluate and compete with these competitors is through the use of better quality information and swift communication.

The second event is the transformation of industrial economies into knowledge economies. With the emergence of the new global knowledge economy, the needs for a transformation in management philosophy, organizational structure, and planning and operation, have also been discussed in some of the previous chapters. Every new generation of human beings are carrying more sophisticated knowledge structures. Emphasis shifts from the tangible to the intangible. Businesses will be producing more and more intangible products. The fastest developing businesses are those that offer knowledge-based services such as consultancy, and research and development (biotechnology). Even for those who are producing physical products, information is assuming a more crucial role. Automation using intelligent machine will be a significant part of the future trend.

Apparently, the two developments mentioned above also indicate that new opportunities can be created through effective use of information and its networks. This is vital in particular to the physical structure of intelligent organizations. Artificial intelligent information systems networks provide the communication means, the connectivity, and the analytical power that are desperately needed by organizations in the new environment. Controlling a widely spread global corporation requires a powerful intelligent information systems network that responds swiftly and reliably at all times. Such a network must be accessible anywhere and at anytime. Basically, intelligent human organizations require a higher quality nervous system.

Vividly, in the new economy, there is an even closer interdependency between intelligent structure on the one hand, and intelligent information systems network on the other. The artificial information systems network forms a significant proportion of the physical structure of an intelligent organization. Therefore, it is interesting to examine the following aspects of intelligent information networks with respect to the concepts developed. Have such networks been developed to the same level of sophistication as nervous systems in intelligent biological beings? Have they attained the status of autopoietic systems? Are current artificial information systems networks supporting the orgmind in the ways they should?

7.2. Intelligent Structure and Artificial Systems

Conceptually, an intelligent organization possesses both a physical structure as well as an intangible deep structure. Embedded in the core of the deep structure of an organization is its orgmind and hence its consciousness. The level of consciousness determines the level of awareness and orgmindfulness. The latter, in turn, is responsible for the collective intelligence and connectivity of the system. It is only when an organization is orgmindful that innovative and creative ideas can emerge from its interacting agents. Thus, a high level of orgmindfulness enhances the collective intelligence of the organization.

Operationally, the connectivity of an organization is highly dependent on the mode of communication. Effective communication helps to create coherent thought. Coherent thought is the social and psychological gel that binds human beings together, and it helps human organizations to achieve functional cohesion more swiftly. A coherent intangible structure supports the physical structure better. Thought technologies such as dialogue and visual thinking have been used to achieve this goal.

In highly intelligent human organizations, the information processing and knowledge creation capabilities of the organizations must be well coupled with the overall intelligent structure. The information systems network together with the intense intelligence source must form the nervous system and the org-brain of an intelligent organization respectively. The connectivity and capability of the natural and artificial systems determine the success in structuring and nurturing intelligent organizations.

As mentioned earlier, the ideal physical structure of intelligent organizations emerges from the deep structure. The physical structure of an intelligent organization possesses three features, namely, an intense intelligence source, an environment scanning and responding component, and an intelligence web. For better continuity, the important characteristics of the three components are summarized below:

a. The existence of an intense intelligence source is vital to all higher levels intelligent systems. This is the brain of the organization. In such composite systems, the org-brain is at least the collection of brains of the interacting agents. The absence of such a source indicates the absence of the leadership node in that organization.

b. A highly intelligent system must also be responsive to its environment. It must act, react and think like any intelligent biological entity. Therefore, the sensing, scanning and responding capabilities of the environmental component are important assets. These are the sensory activities of a biological being. The ability to scan and detect environmental signals coming from environmental targets, the ability to respond to such signals swiftly, and the ability to influence the environmental targets, are vital features of intelligent organizations. For business organizations, the competitive intelligence activities can be substantially enhanced using artificial information systems.

c. Finally, the intelligence web that spreads and permeates the entire system provides the connectivity. This web intertwines and supports all the organizational functions and activities. Through this web, information is communicated, knowledge structures are created and stored, and decisions are disseminated. This is the nervous network of intelligent organizations. The general usage of information and communication technology is vital in this aspect. In particular, the connectivity aspect

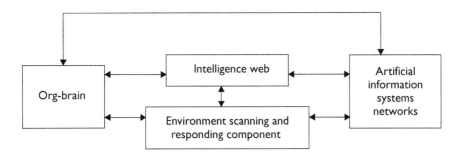

Fig. 7.1. Basic physical nervous structure of an intelligent human organization.

has been greatly enhanced by the e-landscape, wireless technology and multi-media technology.

Apparently, at the physical level, the web and the environmental component can be greatly enhanced by well-integrated artificial information systems networks. Thus, the effectiveness of the latter is closely correlated with the collective intelligence of the organization. Therefore, the mindset of designing an effective artificial intelligent information systems network and integrating it with the natural information network so that the overall information system structure is congruous with the nervous system of highly intelligent organisms is crucial (see Fig. 7.1).

7.3. Internal Intelligent Information Systems

7.3.1. Types of intelligent systems

The intense source is mainly contributed by the human thinking systems. The artificial information systems and their networks that form the intelligent web and the environmental scanning and responding component are the main subsystems of concern in this section. First, the artificial intelligent information systems (IIS) to be examined are broadly classified as internal IIS and external IIS, so that their roles with respect to the web and the environmental component are made more explicit.

The internal IIS in an intelligent organization forms the major portion of its nervous system. This physical network is responsible for processing information, communicating information, creating knowledge structures, and supporting the decision-making processes. It is also the intelligence web that intertwines and supports the economic production system in businesses. The internal intelligent systems are divided into three groups, namely, the traditional information systems, the complexity-based IIS, and the artificial intelligence systems. The traditional information systems have been extensively explained in many sources. In this section, only the latter two classes of systems are briefly introduced.

The external IIS, are mainly the competitive intelligence systems. These systems, the equivalence of the human sensory systems, form mainly the environment scanning and responding component. The early warning systems and data mining systems are discussed. The classification of the current intelligent information systems into the above framework is illustrated in Fig. 7.2.

7.3.2. Complexity-based IIS

Some business organizations are beginning to exploit the unique properties of complexity by capturing them in their information systems. Certain complexity-based algorithms are utilized to process and extract more useful information. For instance, some businesses are using agents and emergent behavior concepts to build information systems to improve their effectiveness in activities such as inventory control, logistics management, and production scheduling. These information systems have helped to reduce costs and add value to the operations of the organizations. The

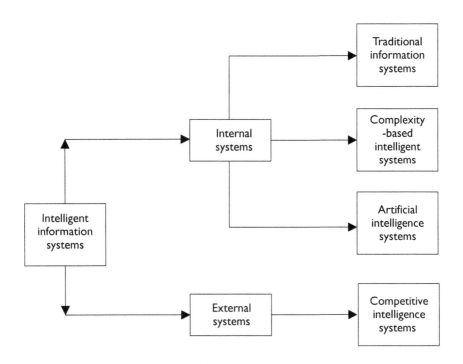

Fig. 7.2. Classification of some intelligent information systems.

following illustrations are examples of complexity-based systems that have been used by some organizations to create an intelligence advantage.

a. *Self-organizing systems*

A self-organizing IIS has been developed by an organization to co-ordinate its painting booths. Each booth is perceived as an independent agent capable of "bidding" on new paint jobs, depending on its ability to perform the work quickly and competitively. The software developed instructs the robots at each paint booth to perform a series of complex tasks. Among other things, the robots treat the surface of the truck with phosphate, apply base coats and clear coats, and set the painted trucks in an oven at a temperature of up to 300 degrees Fahrenheit.

Before the use of the complexity-based system, a single paint booth may have to paint a red truck, then a blue truck, and then a black truck. In this case, paints will have to be changed and machinery cleaned, before each truck can be painted. The new system completely changes the process. If a particular booth has been painting several black trucks consecutively, it will bid to paint any subsequent trucks that are to be painted black. The booth is empowered to decide what it does, or will be doing. This innovative, self-organizing system speeds up the painting process by 50 percent, saves on paint costs, and reduces software requirements by numerous folds.

b. *Genetic algorithm systems*
Another business organization also solved its farm equipment maker's scheduling problems using a complexity-based approach. This time, a survival-of-the-fittest genetic algorithm has been adopted to produce the schedule. Software using the above algorithm allows solutions to emerge, rather than to be calculated.

A computer is used to download data from the plant's database and generates the first set of trial schedules. These schedules are then allowed to "breed", or combine, to create new and improved schedules. Each consecutive schedule is tested for fitness, that is, whether it produces a more efficient throughput than the previous ones generated during that iteration, and the fittest schedules are chosen to integrate with each other to produce even more efficient schedules.

Evolving solutions, rather than engineering solutions, are the essence of such a system. Overnight, schedules close-to-optimal are produced. No worker is involved in the production of the schedules. It is a success as overtime has been reduced, while monthly production figures have increased substantially.

c. *Biodiversity systems*

Yet, another complexity-based system has been developed by a bank to handle portfolio management. The biodiversity system contains risk-management algorithms for swapping currencies and around-the-clock-trading. Instead of a single best solution, the biodiversity system attempts to maintain several near-best approaches to risk management, thereby protecting itself from the intrinsic exposure in a monoculture. The multiple near-best approaches have made portfolio management in this bank safer.

7.3.3. *Artificial intelligence*

Another category of information technology that can elevate the collective intelligence of organizations is artificial intelligence (AI) systems. Compared to the complexity-based technology, the AI technology is much more established. Some AI systems have been in used for several decades. These systems mimic the human mind when processing and consolidating information. These intelligent systems are able to rank tasks and reach conclusions based on previous experiences/training. Thus, they can serve as artificial intelligent nodes in an intelligent structure. Four classes of AI systems, namely, neural networks, expert systems, fuzzy logic systems, and hybrid systems, and their usage are briefly discussed here.

a. *Artificial neural networks*

Artificial neural networks are self-learning systems. These systems learn and teach themselves the set of decision-making rules in the domain in which they operate. The decisions made are based on past experiences. The self-learning ability comes from a self-training mechanism that is embedded within the neural networks. This mechanism also allows the networks to perform analysis on massive amounts of data and tests them for the purpose of finding associations or dependence between data.

For instance, a neural network is used by a military service for the purposes of detecting and cleaning up ordnance. The engineers use the neural network to determine the presence of ordnance that is buried underground. Consequently, due to the higher accuracy of the system, the danger associated with the clearing process is substantially reduced. The intelligent system is able to detect the presence of ordnance, specifying the weight, dimensions, variety and location with high precision.

b. *Expert systems*

The expert systems are another fairly well established AI technology. Expert systems exploit the expertise of experts. The knowledge of expert(s) is mined and stored in the knowledge base which is a crucial component of an expert system. When a problem in the same domain is encountered subsequently, the problem-solving inference engine applies rule-based statements and taps on the knowledge base to draw a conclusion. Thus, the contents embedded in the knowledge base and inference engine determine the performance of an expert system.

An active expert systems technology user is the insurance industry. An advantage of using such systems is that better and more consistent decisions are made. They also enable their users to work faster and with fewer errors. Expert systems are used extensively in processing claims in the insurance industry. Claims processing is an important and difficult task for insurers. Conflicting objectives exist in this area. On the one hand, insurers want to be as responsive and as fast as possible in handling claims in order to give the customers the best service. As most claims are legitimate, the insurer does not want to cause these customers any inconvenience or delay. On the other hand, it is also crucial for the company to identify potential fraudulent claims to be passed on for further investigation. In this respect, a well-designed expert system can help to detect fraud patterns and reveal a potential fraud to the insurers more effectively.

c. *Fuzzy logic systems*
The third type of the AI systems is the fuzzy logic systems. These systems make decisions based on Boolean algebra and probability. Compared to an expert system, a fuzzy logic system is more loosely defined. It incorporates "more or less" statements, and hence is termed "fuzzy". The rules are programmed based on intuitive experience gathered from the domain experts.

A research institution in Singapore and a business organization have jointly developed a fuzzy controller for vacuum furnaces that enable the system to heat turbine components automatically. Previously, operators were needed to adjust the furnace heating, to ensure that the heat transferred by radiation in the furnace would not result in uneven loading conditions. After the adoption of the fuzzy logic system, the adjustment is left to the fuzzy controller, which is intelligent enough to take into account the loading conditions automatically. The implementation of the fuzzy controller leads to higher furnace throughput and reduces both energy consumption and the operator's effort to control the furnace. Each heat treatment cycle, which previously takes 16 hours, is reduced to about 12 hours.

d. *Intelligent hybrid systems*
Owing to the fact that different intelligent techniques are suitable for different applications, intelligent hybrid systems combine two or more techniques to overcome the constraints of the individual techniques, as well as to complement each other. For instance, a fuzzy logic system in loan evaluation can overcome some of its weaknesses by incorporating a neural

network structure to form a system that has the capability to learn fuzzy decision rules automatically.

The strength of intelligent hybrid systems lies in their ability to solve complex problems that are not easily manageable by one type of intelligent system alone. Thus, such systems are powerful tools in the business world. Since the development and applications of these systems are relatively new, not many such tools are in use. An example is a stock exchange system used to carry out detection of insider trading and market manipulation. The system uses a combination of fuzzy logic, neural networks and genetic algorithms to detect suspicious trades that are otherwise extremely difficult to discover in large volumes of trading data.

7.4. External IIS

Business organizations similar to biological systems are open systems that are very much affected by their changing external environment. Therefore, the presence of an effective environment sensing component is critical. The external IIS currently exploited to support this function are mainly the competitive intelligence information systems and data mining systems. Competitive intelligence is an avenue whereby organizations fund, collect, analyze and learn about environmental information that may be advantageous and vital to their survival. It can track competitors' movements, discover profitable opportunities, and open up new markets.

a. *Early warning systems*
Environmental scanning is the organization's ability to monitor or scan the external environment and anticipated changes. The information collected can be strategic as it helps to foster organizational adaptability and survival. For instance, executive information systems (EIS) incorporated with an early warning feature can provide managers with the capability to efficiently

use environmental information when mapping out a strategic plan for the organization.

There are two methods of using EIS for environment scanning, namely the linear approach and the nonlinear approach. The linear approach uses established relationships of environmental factors that have been integrated into the system. The nonlinear or hypermedia approach allows its users to use information in an unstructured manner. These EIS have demonstrated the ability to gather, filter and analyze data, and subsequently communicate information to the appropriate person effectively.

Environmental scanning systems that incorporate expert systems can also better address the needs of strategic planners. These integrated systems simulate the human cognitive processes to enhance environmental scanning by using their machine-learning algorithm and a knowledge base. The environmental scanning process can be expedited through faster recognition of threats and opportunities to the organization. Once relevant environmental issues are identified and prioritized, the organization can move on to determine what other information regarding these issues should be collected and analyzed.

b. *Data mining systems*
Data mining is the process of discovering meaningful correlations and patterns by filtering through large amounts of data. It is the automatic extraction of patterns of information from historical data that enables businesses to focus on the most important aspects of their operation. Data mining and knowledge access have a myriad of applications in many industries. They improve the efficiency and value of an organization by enhancing its knowledge processes. For instance, they are extensively utilized in marketing whereby identifying trends and patterns in a timely manner are critical for success.

Data mining can assist in customer acquisition. Direct marketers apply data mining methods to discover attributes that predict customers' responses to offers and communication programs. Then, the attributes of the customers that the system indicates are most likely to respond are matched with the corresponding attributes of non-customers. The non-customers that are most likely to respond to a new offer or communication are filtered out.

Data mining is also invaluable in customer retention. In a typical application, it identifies those customers who contribute to the company's bottom line but who are likely to leave and go to a competitor. With this information, the company can target these vulnerable customers for special offers and other inducements.

Conversely, in customer abandonment, data mining helps to identify customers who cost more than they contribute. Unprofitable customers populate the files of traditional direct marketers. These are customers that place small orders or habitually order merchandise and then return them. These accounts can be picked out and closed.

7.5. Conclusion

Many human organizations, in particular business organizations, are making a conscientious effort to exploit the potentials of artificial information systems and their networks. Artificial information systems are emerging as an important component of the physical structure of businesses, as well as other human organizations. And these systems have contributed significantly towards the competitiveness of their users in certain manner. Some more innovative organizations are in fact experimenting with newer concepts and technologies which build artificial information systems that are more intelligent and well connected.

However, to date, these artificial systems are not well synchronized or integrated with the structure of the organizations as in highly developed biological organisms. Business organizations and all human organizations in general are not fully aware of themselves as intelligent corporation beings. They are also not aware of the effective role of artificial information systems as nervous systems.

In intelligent organizations, the design and effectiveness of the intelligent information systems network as a component of the nervous system is a critical success factor. A well-developed intelligent information systems web not only helps to strengthen the physical structure, but also provides the means for language to flow better. Therefore, all intelligent organizations must ideally possess a nervous network and sensory system similar to the one in highly intelligent biological organisms. This network must be rightly integrated with the overall structure of the organization and support the operations of the orgmind.

The edge of chaos is where life has enough stability to sustain itself and enough creativity to deserve the name of life. The edge of chaos is where new ideas and innovative genotypes are forever nibbling away at the edges of the status quo, and where even the most entrenched old guard will eventually be overthrown.

Mitchell Waldrop, Complexity

VIII
Interdependency: The Integrated 3C-OK Framework of Intelligence Strategy

This chapter illustrates the interdependency of five significant properties of intelligent human organizations. The properties involved are collective intelligence, connectivity, culture, organizational learning and knowledge management. When structuring and managing intelligent organizations, these properties cannot be considered independently of one another. The 3C-OK framework is introduced to emphasize the fact that complex adaptive systems cannot be analyzed, built or managed using hierarchical decomposition or reductionism. In particular, organizational learning and knowledge management cannot take place effectively in any human organizations without incorporating the other three characteristics. In addition, in highly intelligent organizations, the five properties should function similarly as gluons that confine quarks in elementary particles. Finally, the significance of a mindful culture in intelligent organizations is further reinforced.

8.1. Introduction

At the moment, humanity is situated in the transition period between the third and fourth era in the history of humankind. The world is in the midst of another chaotic transformation, at a new edge of chaos. The primary causes are information explosion, a world population with better knowledge structures, and the need to create higher quality corporate knowledge structures. The increasing use of value information and knowledge called for the creation of a totally different breed of human organizations. The new form of organizations must be able to process information fast, learn fast, use knowledge effectively, adapt to competition and the changing environment swiftly, and evolve successfully. Concurrently, these organizations must also be able to manage interacting agents who are more intelligent (higher awareness) and possess higher quality knowledge structures.

Hence, the flesh strategic approach that focuses on structuring and managing organizations around intelligence has certain advantages. The intellectual development of humanity has arrived at a phase whereby focusing on bio-logic rather than machine-logic makes better sense. The design and strength of biological systems is far more superior to that of mechanistic models. Machines have to be controlled, monitored and maintained externally. Biological systems inherently manifest properties of the complexity theory.

Human beings are biological beings. People are not merely a physical means of production. More importantly, each human being carries a nonlinear thinking system from which many other properties and features of that creature are defined and determined. Connecting people is thus linking these highly complex thinking systems together to form an effective composite system that is organism-like and not machine-like. To better manage human organizations, the human thinking systems and their dynamic must be better handled. Voluntary collaboration can only be achieved through mutual respect, intimacy, subtlety and trust. Thus, the current social/corporate culture must be transformed. Leaders of all forms of human organizations must be prepared to make the paradigmatic shift and venture into a new dimension if their leadership is to remain effective, relevant and acceptable.

In this chapter, the 3C-OK framework (encompassing collective intelligence, connectivity, culture, organizational learning and knowledge management), a significant integrated tool of intelligence strategy is introduced. It is a critical component of the intelligent organization theory. A vital aspect of this framework is the recognition of the interdependency of the five attributes involved. The interdependent and nonlinear aspect of these five attributes is a vital characteristic in the dynamic of intelligent human organizations. This characteristic reveals how an organization can be managed more effectively. For instance, knowledge management activity cannot be carried out in an organization without cautiously managing the other four activities concurrently.

8.2. The 3C (Collective Intelligence, Connectivity and Culture) Dynamic

8.2.1. Consciousness, connectivity and collective intelligence

The universe is conscious and so are some of its microcosms. Consciousness is an extremely unique attribute that exists in this world and it entices some of the best minds that existed. The level of consciousness spreads over a spectrum. It has been stated in earlier chapters that arising from human consciousness are two mental functions, namely, awareness and mindfulness. Awareness focuses outwards. It recognizes the environment in which the individual exists and enables the latter to act/react to the changing circumstances. On the other hand, mindfulness focuses inwards. It executes internal search on the mind and also observes the mental state of the mind. Mindfulness can help the mind to watch itself when a new thought emerges. In this respect, mindfulness only emerges from a highly conscious source.

Similar to a human being, an intelligent organization must be aware of its environment and orgmindful of its orgmind. This fundamental concept is stipulated in Axiom I of the 3C-OK framework as follows:

Axiom I

An intelligent human organization manifests both awareness and orgmindfulness, and they are mental functions that emerge from consciousness.

When the consciousness-connectivity cycle is analyzed, an orgmind and its collective intelligence appears to be an inevitable feature embedded in all intelligent organizations. A high level of consciousness and quality connectivity are necessary to create and sustain a high level of collective intelligence. In return, a high collective intelligence will further enhance the group's consciousness and connectivity. The element ensuring that this cycle flows smoothly is orgmindfulness. It must be emphasized that orgmindfulness is the organizational mental function that nurtures a high level of collective intelligence. Thus, collective intelligence and the consciousness-connectivity cycle are mutually enhancing. This intrinsic characteristic is stipulated as the next axiom:

Axiom II

A highly intelligent human organization possesses a high level of collective intelligence that drives a better and more effective evolutionary dynamic.

The consciousness-connectivity cyclical dynamic is also responsible for establishing other vital attributes such as mindset, culture, vision, as well as decision-making processes, in human organizations. The elements that ensure the effectiveness of the above creations are again awareness and orgmindfulness.

In addition, arising from the analysis of the consciousness-connectivity cycle, it is recognized that an organization can remain stable only if its level/quality of connectivity exceeds its increasing complexity. Once the latter characteristic dominates, the system will move towards the edge of chaos and eventually falls into the chaotic state, if the degree of freedom becomes too large. However, if complexity is skillfully exploited, re-structuring will take place through evolution, emergence and dissipation. In this case, the system moves into a higher state of existence, and a battle is won.

In this respect, corresponding to the consciousness-connectivity cycle is the emergence-dissipation cycle. This is another self-organizing cycle that an intelligent organization will venture into if a sufficient level of collective intelligence is attained. This is the cycle that helps to modify/ enhance the structure. It is important to note again that the presence of structure indicates the presence of information, and vice-versa. All forms of structure are created by intelligence. As complexity increases, a higher level of intelligence is needed to process information or visualize structure in the system. Thus, a more sophisticated structure in human organizations can only be attained if the above two cycles are integrated, and evolve simultaneously.

The merging of the two cycles helps to create order/structure out of complexity. The macro-cycle is the dynamic that supports the evolution of complex adaptive systems. It is the desire to survive in a more complex environment that leads to the evolution of all biological organisms. In this situation, greater order is established out of a higher level of complexity. This analysis reiterates that consciousness, connectivity, complexity, emergence and dissipation are indeed the most vital properties of all complex adaptive systems, including human organizations. The interrelationship of the five abstract attributes is illustrated in Fig. 8.1. It provides a better perspective for explaining and comprehending the abstract dynamic of intelligent human complex adaptive systems and the bio-logic of living systems driven by intelligence, on a macroscopic level.

Consequently, the model further supports the fact that all forms of human organizations are composite complex adaptive systems because their constituents, the human thinking systems, are themselves complex adaptive systems. The complex and adaptive dynamics of such systems will vary with time, depending on changes in attributes/entities such as memberships, interacting processes, and external environment. And understanding the five core properties of chaos and their integrated dynamic is a significant knowledge that leaders and managers must acquire in the current context and for future usage.

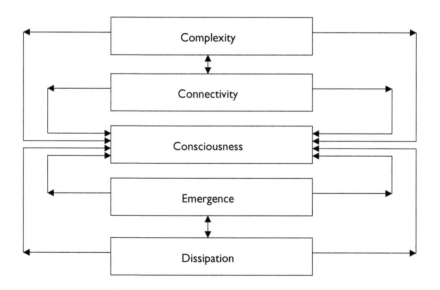

Fig. 8.1. The interactive dynamic of the five core properties of chaos theory.

8.2.2. *Mindful culture*

The vital mental function steering the dynamic of the above cycle is mindfulness. As stipulated earlier, mindfulness is the attribute that directs the human mind to focus internally. Most human beings today are more concerned about the environment rather than the internal mental state of the mind itself. This mindset is incomplete and disastrous. Both mindfulness and awareness are significant attributes that affect autopoiesis and self-organization. The two mental functions must be executed concurrently. They are equally important to the evolution and co-evolution of an interacting agent and its system.

When a mind is mindful, it learns faster, and it learns more effectively. Such a mind also erects higher quality knowledge structures. This characteristic has been stipulated in the intelligent person model. Logical and effective theories and better decision-making processes only originate from a mind that is mindful. Under all circumstances, mindfulness is a crucial attribute in all highly intelligent minds. Mindfulness also helps to elevate collective intelligence and establish better connectivity. Thus, it is a greatly desirable attribute that must be nurtured by all intelligent human beings.

Similarly, an organization that is orgmindful learns faster through sharing knowledge. With the right mindset, all interacting agents in such an organization believe that the continuous acquisition of knowledge and skills is their individual responsibility. They are also more willing to share whatever they have acquired. Such a collaborative and supportive culture that increases the survival ability of the organization only emerges from an orgmind that is orgmindful. A highly orgmindful organization can also more quickly self-organizes when the need arises. Thus, the ability to maintain a high level of orgmindfulness is a new intelligence advantage. However, today, most organizations are still more outward seeking and they tend to neglect or ignore the internal mental state of the interacting agents.

Therefore, to nurture collective intelligence, enhance connectivity, and cultivate a mindful culture more efficiently, the orgmind must first be orgmindful. Concurrently, a corporate culture that is more willing to collaborate and share, and is more concern of the corporation's vision and mission, will emerge. In addition, the internal reflecting activity of the orgmind must be sustainable and continuous. Continuity is a crucial requirement as both the external and internal environments are changing at all times.

A mindful culture can only be cultivated through continuous refinement using orgmindfulness. And an intelligent organization is regarded as highly intelligent only if a mindful culture exists. Apparently, nurturing a mindful culture prepares the organization for better self-organization and hence support the emergent strategy more effectively. Without a mindful culture, human organizations today will not be able to withstand the current rapid changing environment. In this respect, an organization that is always orgmindful and coupled with awareness is a better survivor. In addition, it must be noted that the equilibrium in this respect is dynamic. This conceptualization is stipulated as the next axiom:

Axiom III
A mindful culture exits in all intelligent human organizations. It supports the system objectives as well as the requirements of the individual interacting agents (that is, it supports both the evolution and co-evolution dynamics, and the autopoietic and self-organizing dynamics).

8.2.3. *Quality corporate intelligent enhancer*

On a more microscopic perspective, the collective intelligence of a human organization can be nurtured and enhanced by directing attention on the corporate intelligence enhancer. As the environment becomes more and more complex, this enhancer, located in the orgmind, must be able to constantly provide the organization with higher and higher levels of organizing ability.

Similar to that in an individual thinking system, the corporate intelligent enhancer is a triad comprising three entities, namely, collective intelligence, corporate knowledge structure, and corporate theory and philosophy (see Fig. 8.2). The dynamic of the enhancer is facilitated by at least one physical symbol system manifested in a more advanced form as a language. Language when used rightly is a social glue that binds all the human thinking systems in an organization. A highly developed and effective language is a product of both mindfulness and orgmindfulness.

The content of the intelligence enhancer highlights the significant of a corporate knowledge structure in the new environment. The presence of a physical symbol system enables externalized knowledge

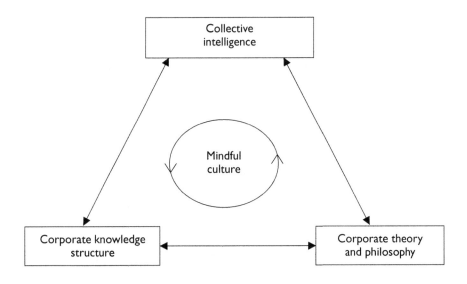

Fig. 8.2. The corporate intelligence enhancer.

structures to be constructed in human organizations. As the interaction between knowledge structure and theory determines whether a new piece of information is consumed or rejected, a better-organized knowledge structure together with a better-developed theory will facilitate the consumption of more pieces of information, or the better use of a new piece of information. Apparently, the value of a new piece of information depends on the quality of the knowledge structure and the collective intelligence space of the organization. In this respect, the presence of a quality enhancer boosts the decision-making processes of human organizations.

8.3. The OK (Organizational Learning and Knowledge Management) Dynamic

8.3.1. *Organizational learning, knowledge structure and mindful culture*

Learning occurs at different levels in an organization. Individual learning is the primary level of learning in any organization, whether the latter is a family, community, business corporation or nation. This learning process should be encouraged and rewarded if humankind is to continue to exist on this planet. However, to be collectively intelligent, the group as a whole must also learn. Thus, higher-level learning must occur simultaneously if the group aspires to compete as a team. In this respect, learning must take place concurrently and spontaneously at different levels as intelligent organizations of different sizes emerge.

A competitive and intelligent organization must be able to learn faster than its competitors. Otherwise, it is not really that intelligent relatively. Collective intelligence is responsible for carrying out the learning process in human organization. Analogous to intelligence in an individual human being, collective intelligence is the driving force behind learning in intelligent organizations. As mentioned earlier, orgmindfulness and awareness are the crucial mental functions that influence the dynamic of the autopoietic and self-organizing processes, and hence the rate of learning in organization. Thus, without a mindful culture, organization learning can never be optimized. The continuous learning ability of an intelligent organization is stipulated as the next axiom:

Axiom IV

An intelligent organization possesses a continuous learning ability that enables it to consume new information, adapt to changing environment, make better decision, and evolve with time.

There are some differences between individual and organizational learning. As an organization learns, knowledge accumulates and the latter has to be stored physically. The accumulation of corporate knowledge is a highly significant function of intelligent organizations. Corporate knowledge structures do not only reside in the mind of the interacting agents alone. Intelligent organizations have to create additional corporate knowledge structures outside the traditional human thinking systems. Usually, these externalized knowledge structures are stored in external physical storages. Information and communications technology has to be exploited in this respect. An organized approach is essential to move towards optimality. Plan and strategy must be mapped out to ensure that an organization learns faster and better, and accumulates and utilizes knowledge more effectively. Inevitably, organizational learning and knowledge management are vital activities that must be highly integrated in intelligent organizations.

8.3.2. Types of knowledge

At the frontier of knowledge activity is the creation of new knowledge. Only top-notch researchers and highly creative people are involved in this activity. The second line of action is the acquisition of knowledge. The acquisition of knowledge, re-organizing it, giving it a new perspective, and using it innovatively to solve a problem and make a better decision, are the daily tasks of many professors, managers and national leaders. However, as humankind ventures deeper into the intelligence era, the acquisition and utilization of knowledge at all levels has become a necessity. Eventually, every individual will have to participate in such an activity in this highly competitive world.

Information first enters the thinking system of the individual human beings usually with the support of one or more physical symbols systems. It appears that knowledge is always made tacit before becoming explicit. In this respect, the knowledge created or acquired by the individuals has to be extracted and disseminated, if it is to be made valuable to others. Otherwise, it will remain within the thinking system that acquired it, that is, it is only useful for the individuals' usage and consumption.

In intelligent human organizations, it is essential to make the tacit and internalized knowledge explicit. In the new environment, having experts alone is not sufficient to operate effectively. It is vital to have experts that are willing to share their expertise. However, the tacit and internalized knowledge structures, as well as innovative ideas, are individual intellectual properties. To get the members of an organization to share/collaborate voluntarily, the corporate culture must be right. Again, the presence of a mindful culture is crucial. The knowledge to manage knowledge must be present.

With the introduction of the knowledge-based/expert systems technology, human organizations begun to realize the significant of externalized knowledge. After the construction of the first artificial automated knowledge structure, the domain of knowledge management has evolved substantially. Knowledge repositories have proliferated to certain extent, continuous updating and usage of these artificial knowledge structures has become a necessity in knowledge-intensive organizations. Therefore, with the even greater dependency on better knowledge to survive the future competition, the quality of knowledge structures and knowledge management processes must be enhanced. Similar to an intelligent being, this is one activity that no intelligent organization can avoid.

8.3.3. *Quality knowledge structure and knowledge management process*

The quality knowledge structure embedded in the individual human thinking system has to be updated through continuous learning. The current emphasis is on fast learning coupled with innovation and creativity. Many developed nations are moving their education and skills training systems towards this direction. The objective is to develop quality knowledge structures in their people. These individuals' knowledge structures are the most vital sources for establishing quality organizational knowledge structure.

A high level of collective intelligence is the main element for driving quality knowledge management processes in intelligent human organizations. The two critical quantities, collective intelligence and individuals' knowledge structures, are intangibles and they cannot be acquired by force. As indicated earlier, a new form of relationship has to be established. In this case, a mindful culture is an essential facilitating medium. An intelligent organization and its interacting agents must work collaboratively as partners, orchestrated by a new form of leadership and management philosophy. People with highly sophisticated knowledge structures cannot be led or managed in the present manner.

As the world population becomes more educated and better informed, the values of people may be modified. Monetary rewards alone may not be sufficient. Social recognition and mutual respect could be a new perspective that must be satisfied. The need of intangible satisfaction of the individuals has increased. Thus, intelligent organizations must also recognize this new trend. Otherwise, the organizational learning and knowledge management dynamic will not evolve satisfactorily or spontaneously. The presence of the knowledge management dynamic in intelligent organizations is stated in the next axiom:

Axiom V
An intelligent organization possesses the ability to create and enhance corporate knowledge structures as the organizational learning dynamic progresses.

As the value of a piece of information coming into an organization depends on the quality of the knowledge structures already established, quality corporate knowledge structure is a new critical success factor in the knowledge economy. Effective knowledge management dynamic is another new critical success factor. Apparently, contributing to corporate knowledge structures as well as exploiting existing structures is equally important. The effective combination of the two factors together with organizational learning and the efficient use of appropriate theory constitute an intelligent advantage that human organizations must exploit in the knowledge-intensive environment.

8.4. The Integrated 3C-OK Dynamic

The interdependency of collective intelligence, connectivity and culture (3C), and organizational learning and knowledge management

(OK), and their dynamic clearly indicates that intelligent organization must be managed differently from the present approach. The 3C-OK framework illustrated that the attributes governing the interaction of human beings are integrated. These attributes in human organizations cannot be decomposed and focused on separately as a linear system is often dealt with. Collective intelligence, culture, connectivity, organizational learning and knowledge management are intertwined in a complex manner, and together with the processes involved they form a complex adaptive system.

The situation must be analogous to the confinement of quarks in elementary particles. For instance, a proton has three quarks. They are interlocked in the proton and cannot be separated by gluons. In addition, the gluons behave in a nonlinear manner. When the quarks are moved apart, the attractive force of the gluons increase in strength. The strength increases quickly, thus confining the quarks to the elementary particles. Similarly, when some of the above organizational attributes in human systems are diminished, their presence becomes even more necessary. The more a particular attribute is being removed, the greater its presence is needed. In this respect, the 3C-OK helps to glue the interacting agents together. They are the gluons in all human organizations. In addition, they must also be able to bind certain interacting agents more strongly when needed.

Thus, recognizing that these five attributes are interdependent and they are the gluons of human organizations, and that their dynamic is complex and nonlinear, is a new mindset that is crucial to the structuring and management of human organizations in the intelligence era. Therefore, the 3C-OK framework is a significant component of the intelligence strategy. The framework points a new direction in leadership and management philosophy. Interacting agents with highly sophisticated knowledge structures must be managed differently. The dynamic of the 3C-OK dynamic is summarized in Fig. 8.3.

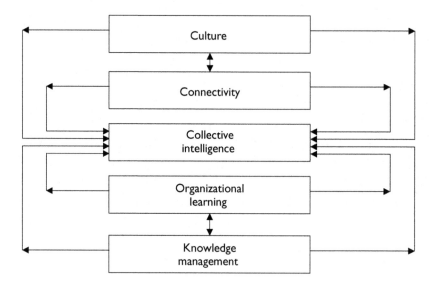

Fig. 8.3. The integrated 3C-OK dynamic of intelligent organizations.

8.5. Conclusion

Apparently, the five core properties of chaos theory constitute an excellent macroscopic platform for analyzing, comprehending, organizing, leading and managing all intelligent human organizations in the new environment. The dynamic of this set of properties together with some additional observations from the complexity theory further reinforces the fact that intelligent human organizations are composite complex adaptive systems.

The interdependency characteristic of complex adaptive systems in intelligent human organizations is captured in the 3C-OK framework. The key factors of the integrated framework are summarized as below:

a. The five associated attributes of intelligent organizations, namely, collective intelligence, connectivity, culture, organizational learning and knowledge management are highly interdependent on each other. They are also the gluons of highly intelligent human organizations. Together with the dynamic involved, they formed a composite complex adaptive system.

b. Thus, in particular, organizational learning and knowledge management cannot take place effectively in any human organizations without the presence of high collective intelligence, quality connectivity, and a supportive mindful culture. Consequently, orgmindfulness must be allocated higher priority. It only emerges in organizations with a very high level of consciousness.

c. Finally, recognizing the confinement effect of 3C-OK in all human organizations is an essential mindset for all current/potential leaders and managers. The 3C-OK framework is an important reference source for leading and managing intelligent organizations more effectively as humankind moves deeper into the intelligence paradigm.

Watching the river that day the boy made a discovery. It was not the discovery of a material thing, something he might put his hand upon. He could not even see it. He had discovered an idea. Quite suddenly, yet quietly, he knew that everything in his life would someday pass under the bridge and be gone, like water.

Grove Patterson, Toledo Blade

IX
Towards a Higher Order of Existence

The chapter concludes the book by providing a more holistic and integrated view of the intelligent organization theory through recollecting the various perspectives involved. Organizing around intelligence is the strategy to adopt in the current environment. This paradigmatic shift in mindset is inevitable. Certain properties of complex adaptive systems have been exploited by businesses in the US and Europe. (Please refer to the bibliography.) However, the intelligent organization theory conceived and developed in this book contains some fresh concepts and ideas. One aspect is the interdependency of the five properties of intelligent organizations that is captured in the 3C-OK framework. Another is the intelligent person model. It may not be too extreme to note that a highly intelligent human organization is one whose interacting agents are mostly intelligent persons as defined in this theory.

9.1. Introduction

As humankind ventures into a new millennium, and the whole world becomes better informed and educated, many dimensions of the human world will be undergoing great transformation. What was accepted as traditional or heritage may now be regarded as out-dated or obsolete. The evolution dynamic and outputs will change as the inputs vary. The rules and environment that were once logical or bearable may now be totally incongruous. Ultimately, economic abundance and the quality of human existence may not be positively correlated. Even industrialization and human/societal development may no more be synonymous.

The crucial changes in input that will affect humankind as mentioned at the beginning of this book are re-captured in Fig. 9.1. With respect to organizing, managing and leading human organizations, these changes vividly indicate the importance of intelligence as the utmost priority. Organizing around intelligence is the first strategic principle to adopt. For all human organizations, regardless of their sizes and missions, the fundamental aim is to make themselves more intelligent. And the structure, management and leadership of intelligent human organizations are very different from the current forms and practices.

9.2. Holistic Perception

The intelligence paradigm encompasses a fresh mindset and a new direction that focuses on organizing around intelligence. The different perspectives of organizing around intelligence are briefly re-captured here to ensure that the readers nurture and attain a more holistic view of the intelligent organization theory. The primary focal point of this approach is the human mind and the orgmind.

Individual level:

a. Focus on elevating the awareness and mindfulness of the individual minds continuously.

b. Enhance the learning processes and knowledge structures of the interacting agents.

Organizational level:

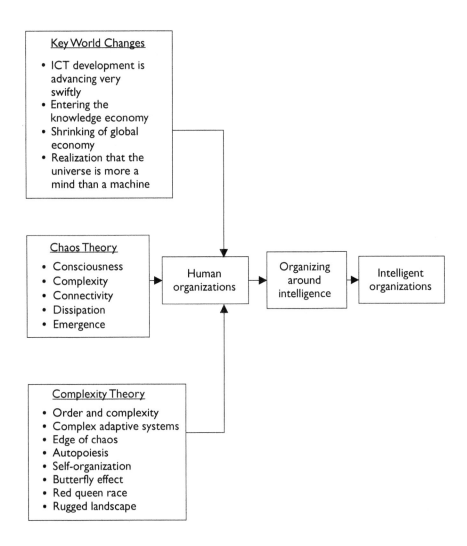

Fig. 9.1. Critical inputs that are overwhelming human organizations and a transformation in mindset is inevitable.

a. Focus on elevating the collective intelligence of the system.

b. Be orgmindful, that is, be aware of the mental state of the interacting agents at all times.

c. Ensure fast continuous organizational learning and enhancement of corporate knowledge structures.

d. Nurture better connectivity and a more mindful culture.

This perspective of organizing around intelligence will eventually lead to the enhancement of other properties, characteristics and activities such as the intelligence enhancer, evolution and co-evolution, and the new form of leadership and management strategy as summarized in Fig. 9.2.

The next aspect of organizing around intelligence is the structural perspective. Similar to any highly intelligent biological beings the intelligent structure of human organizations has three components. The orgmind is the center of the intelligent structure. It can be created through mind fusion. Thus, it is at least a collection of the minds of the interacting agents in the system. The orgmind drives the dynamic of the intangible structure that encompasses numerous properties and activities as illustrated in Fig. 9.3. The third component is the physical structure. Ideally, the details of the latter should emerge from the dynamic of the intangible structure.

The third perspective is the complex, adaptive and nonlinear aspect of intelligent organizations. This dimension has been covered fairly substantially in the earlier chapters. Fig. 9.4 below re-captures some of the key focuses of this analysis. A significant area that must be allocated special attention is the edge of chaos. This is the space where unknown amount of innovation and creativity are embedded, awaiting the right decoders. This unexplored space contains "survival nuggets" that have not been mined. Equally significant is the intelligent organization dynamic that emerges from the integration of autopoiesis and self-organization. A high level of collective intelligence and orgmindfulness give rise to better self-organization. A highly intelligent organization with better emergent strategy will survive better at a punctuation point.

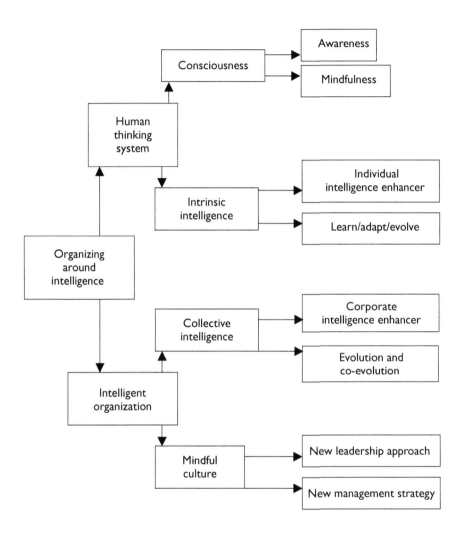

Fig. 9.2. The primary focus of organizing around intelligence that concentrates on intelligence and collective intelligence.

The last perspective concentrates on the intelligence-associated strategic model/plan. The three models introduced in this book are the intelligent person model, the 3C-OK framework, and the intelligent organization strategic plan that encompasses both the

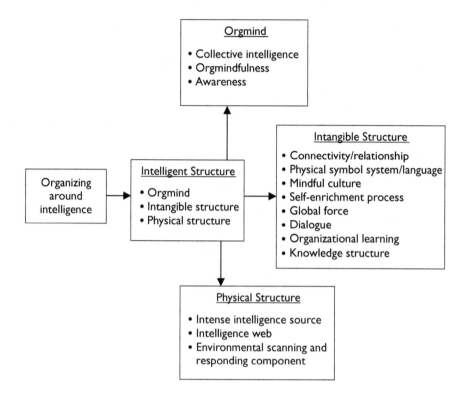

Fig. 9.3. The basic structural aspect of organizing around intelligence.

deliberate and emergent characteristics of complex adaptive systems. Briefly, it is interesting to note that the intelligent person model focuses on the mindset of the interacting agents that has three fundamental characteristics as stated in Chapter 8. Next, the 3C-OK framework emphasizes the interdependency of the five properties of human complex adaptive systems. Changes in one characteristic will affect the rest in one way or another.

Finally, the deliberate and emergent aspect of intelligence strategy is a significant observation. It indicates that strategic planning or planning in general is not totally structured. A plan cannot be a

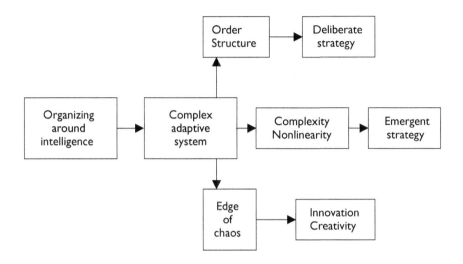

Fig. 9.4. The perspective that focuses on human organizations as intelligent complex adaptive systems and their properties.

detailed procedure whereby individual steps are clearly specified and must be fully observed. In fact, an emergent component must always be included. The emergent component may merely indicate a new direction that arises from new thinking, analysis and observation. However, its role is vital as the organization may encounter punctuation points over time. In this respect, the system will be able to respond intelligently to the unexpected changing conditions. Some details of this approach are re-captured in Fig. 9.5.

In order to achieve a more in-depth understanding of the intelligent organization theory, the four perspectives are re-visualized separately above. However, it is vital to reinforce that the various perspectives are highly interdependent too. There is a substantial amount of overlapping in the four approaches. This is the basic nature of complexity theory, as well as the intelligent organization theory. When analyzing an intelligent organization an integrative

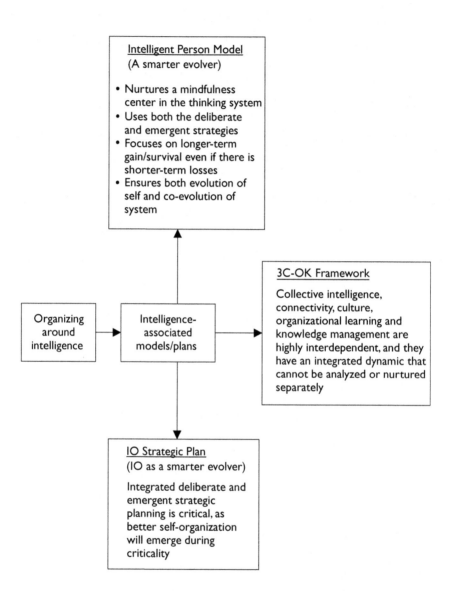

Fig. 9.5. The intelligence-associated model/plan for leading and managing intelligent human organizations.

analysis is inevitable. Thus, when structuring, managing and leading an intelligent organization, a holistic understanding and application of the theory is necessary. Intelligent organizations cannot be constructed overnight. An intelligent organization can only be nurtured holistically through gradual evolvement, that is, through emergence and dissipation, and concurrently looking out for punctuation points. This is the intelligence paradigm.

9.3. The Wisdom Paradigm

Anyone who aspires to be an expert in this domain or any other disciplines must realize that there is no shortcut to meeting the ambition. A tremendous amount of hard work is needed. Effort is the root of all achievements. Interest and self-motivation are the other two crucial factors. Probably, this requirement is fairly obvious. In addition, the knowledge structures in the mind of the individual must be substantially nurtured/internalized and their quality must be continuously enriched. A fair amount of time is essential. Basically, the learner must have executed the following activities:

a. Must know the fundamentals of the domain (which are very unlikely to change in the near future) very well.

b. Must acquire the skills of problem solving, understanding in depth, and independent learning in the domain.

c. Must be aware of the new directions that are emerging in the domain.

With respect to increasing the quality of the knowledge structures and improving one's journey to be an expert, the following questions must also be positively achieved:

a. How large is your knowledge chunk size?

b. How fast are you able to recognize patterns in a sea of information?

c. How fast are you able to link recognized patterns to a problem and its solution?

Fundamentally, quality knowledge structures must be present before innovation and creativity can emerge. A new discovery or invention only emerges from a prepared mind. Thus, humankind can only sustain its existence through the creation of new knowledge.

Finally, it may also be beneficial to note that a promising learner is one that has the potential to overtake the teacher. And a great teacher is one that possesses the ability to stimulate a learner to surpass oneself. Nobody lives forever. Therefore, every new generation must move on to unexplored frontiers, edges of chaos, generate and exploit new knowledge, and adopt a new form of structure and philosophy; a higher level of existence.

Appendix: Chaos/Complexity/ Complex Adaptive Systems

1. Order and Chaos

In human organizations both linear order and chaos intertwine in varying degrees and alternate throughout the life history of the systems. A period of relative order is followed by a period of "chaos", which in turn brings forth a new order (usually with a more complex structure).

The period of chaos is a natural and necessary part of development/ evolution of nonlinear dynamical systems. Over time, it arises at the bifurcation point of discontinuous change. The conditions for the creation of new order are born out of the turbulence of chaos.

2. What Is Chaos?

Chaos is the study of dynamical systems. Dynamical systems can be visualized in two different ways.

a. Dynamical Systems:

- Can be linear, closed conservative systems.

- Can be dissipative, open, nonlinear systems.

b. Dynamical Systems:

- Contain a set of processes (dynamic), and

- Contain a set of states (outcomes).

Chaos is a process. It is dynamic. Thus, chaos is a type of dynamical phenomenon that happens when the state of a system changes with time. Hence, chaos is not a state.

3. What Is Order?

Linear order, certainty, regularity, reliability, predictability and similarity do exist in this world. Within certain time scales and under certain conditions many phenomena change in an orderly, linear way. For most people, order provides comfort, confidence and assurance.

In linear systems, small causes have small effects and large causes have large effects. Two similar systems under the same conditions often develop/evolve in the same way/manner. Under most circumstances, small errors in measurements cancel each other and are negligible in predicting outcomes. From the ways the system changed in the past, it is often possible to predict how the system will change in the future. This is the world of the exact sciences.

4. Linearity and Nonlinearity

The essence of linearity is the proportionate relationship between cause and effect. In a nonlinear system, the directly proportional relationship is no longer true (nonlinearity). Consequently, in a non-linear system, starting points that are almost the same may evolve into completely different ending points.

5. Sensitive to Initial Conditions

Lorenz had demonstrated that in many systems, there are variables that either cannot be measured exactly, or if they can be measured, the slightest initial difference, if amplified repeatedly, may lead to unpredictable consequence. This phenomenon of repetitive amplification is due to iteration (nonlinear feedback loop) in complex systems. The sensitive to initial conditions of complex systems is given the term butterfly effect. This is a deviation from the understandings of the exact sciences.

6. Interdependency

Nonlinearity and sensitive dependence on initial conditions alone are not enough to create chaotic conditions in systems. Chaos develops in nonlinear systems that also exhibit interdependency.

Nonlinearity is not the same as interdependent. Nonlinearity deals with dis-proportionality. Interdependent deals with the relationships between systems and the way they affect one another. For instance, in human organizations interdependency is related to connectivity and culture.

7. Far-from-Equilibrium States

Far-from-equilibrium systems do not return to their regular state, they never repeat themselves and they are nonlinear.

The nonlinear interactions in far-from-equilibrium open systems allow the systems to pass from one basic state to another in discontinuous transitions.

Far-from-equilibrium in nonlinear interdependent systems is both the source of chaos and renewal.

The dynamics of human systems that are nonlinear, far-from-equilibrium and interdependent are in permanent flux that includes a phase of chaos, self-organization and renewal.

Life is built on the basis of far-from-equilibrium changes.

8. Complex Adaptive Systems

In complex adaptive systems, both order and complexity (deterministic chaos) co-exist.

A complex adaptive system comprises a group of dynamically changing and interactive heterogeneous agents. The group of human thinking systems in a human organization forms a complex adaptive system.

A complex adaptive system is an open system in perpetual motion. For instance, an interacting agent can join or leave an organization at any moment.

Even the set of rules governing its dynamic is evolving/changing.

New information is continuously consumed (adaptive) as the system tries to adapt by self-organizing and/or co-evolving. Its ability to anticipate, respond to, and influence the change in environmental conditions is vital, as a slight variation in initial conditions can lead to a totally unpredictable global outcome (butterfly effect).

9. States of Complex Adaptive Systems

- Point attractor (Feigenbaum number between 0 to 2).
  (The system is attracted to a fixed point.)

- Periodic state (above 2, less than 3).
  (The same behavior is repeated over and over again.)

- Strange attractor (3 to below 3.7).
  (It has some kind of patterned order and boundary, likes an infinite line/curve that never goes through the same point twice but continues indefinitely within a bounded space.)

- Chaotic state (3 and above)
  (When Feigenbaum number=3.7 and above, the system becomes chaotic, has infinite numbers degree of freedom, and is extremely difficult to analyze.)

10. Self-Organization

Nonlinear, interdependent, far-from-equilibrium system continuously self-organizes (spontaneous—order for free) itself into a new, more complex order.

Self-organization is the principle underlying the emergence of forms manifest in physical, chemical, biological, ecological, social and cultural structures.

With self-organization, matter becomes active and has the potential to spontaneously and unpredictably develop new forms and structures by itself.

It is also the principle connecting the sciences of the physical (non-living) world and the world of the living (biological).

11. Bifurcation

On the way to a new order, a complex adaptive system passes through a period of great instability. It is faced with decision points on which its future will depend. A variety of different paths are opened up before the system. Which path it chooses at each of these forking/branching points determines the possibilities open to it in the future. Different path may lead to a completely different direction and entirely different ways of self-organizing itself. These points of choice are called bifurcations.

12. Connectivity and Relationships

Another basic characteristic of complex adaptive systems is connectivity (relationships). In the world of complex adaptive systems, everything is connected to everything else, for instance, business corporations and economy, economies and the global society.

A human organization becomes more robust when it has a more complex structure. But, the more numerous are the fluctuations that threaten its stability. To maintain its wholeness—despite discontinuous changes—it has to invest in itself more meaningful communication and effective relationships between its components, as well as between itself and its environment. Thus, the quality of its connectivity is vital.

The indicators of complexity are the degree of differentiation and degree of organization in terms of intricacy of connectedness.

When human systems lag in matching the quality of their relationships to the degree of complexity of these relationships, they are in for a period of great uncertainty. Increasing complexity of a system breeds growing uncertainty when it is not matched with a parallel change in the quality of relationships.

To ensure the survival of the system, the quality of relationships must be greater than the degree of complexity.

13. The Edge of Chaos

Complexity arises as a natural/inherent development when a complex adaptive system reaches a certain level of variety and diversity. Internal processes of autocatalysis feed the system leading it to self-organize into a more complex level of functioning. If the complexity of the interactions is rich enough then the system becomes supercritical. The autocatalytic process would be inevitable, and the system would get order for free.

In this respect, all complex adaptive systems evolve over time to the edge of chaos. This is the state where the system needs to balance itself so as not to fall into too much chaos on the one hand, and too much order on the other.

Systems at the edge of chaos are stable enough to receive and keep information, while they are also able to transmit them. They can adjust themselves to a point where their computational ability is maximized. This is also the point where they attain their highest level of fitness and adaptability.

It is also at the edge of chaos that organizations are most innovative and creative.

The Santa Fe Institute raises the following possibilities for complex adaptive systems at the edge of chaos.

- They are best able to function adaptively.

- They have the highest fitness.

- They can perform complex computations best.

- They learn to acquire the basic competency of evolution.

- They have the widest range of behaviors.

- They are able to function effectively in a fast changing environment.

- They have a rich choice of alternatives.

Glossary

Adaptive: It is the ability to consume new information and to react to changes spontaneously.

Attractor: It is the state of a dynamical system.

Autopoiesis: It is closely associated with individuality. It is the inward center-seeking dynamic that resists changes and makes communication difficult.

Awareness: It is a primary mental function that arises from human consciousness. A high level of consciousness leads to a high level of awareness of a self and its surrounding environment.

Butterfly effect: The output state of a complex system can be highly sensitive to the conditions of the input state, thus rendering the output highly unpredictable. This characteristic is known as the butterfly effect. In this respect, a small input can lead to an enormous output.

Chaos: It is the process/dynamical phenomenon that causes a complex system to enter the chaotic state.

Chaos theory: This is the popular name for the theory of dynamical systems.

Chaotic: The state whereby the details cannot be understood and there is no obvious global pattern.

Co-evolution: It indicates the emergent and survival of two or more complex adaptive systems concurrently. The concept focuses on connectivity and the relationships between/among the systems.

Complex: The state whereby the details cannot be comprehended but patterns that enable the system as a whole to be understood are present.

Complex adaptive systems: These are complex systems that consume information and respond/adapt to changes continuously. Consequently, they are more predictable than complex systems that are not adaptive.

Complex systems: All complex systems are highly unpredictable and what can be predicted is very constraint.

Complexity theory: It is the theory of complex adaptive systems and it focuses on the edge of chaos.

Connectivity: It is the quality of the relationships among interacting agents (human beings) in a system (human organization), as well as the quality of the relationships between a complex adaptive system and its environment.

Consciousness: Consciousness is the most fundamental/significant phenomenon of the human mind, as the other mental factors cannot exist without it. Consciousness enables the mind to cognize the world of thoughts and ideas through the two primary functions of awareness and mindfulness.

Dialogue: It is a methodology of thought technology invented by a group of researchers at MIT.

Dissipation: It is the removal of extra entropy from a complex system that is undergoing emergence.

Dissipative structure: A stable structure with recognizable form and is continually being dissipated and renewed.

Edge of chaos: It is a state of bounded instability in complex systems and it exists between the states of order and disorder. When complex adaptive systems are at the edge of chaos their computational ability is maximized, and the systems are at their highest level of fitness and adaptability. The edge of chaos is more a space rather than an edge.

Emergence: It is the production of global patterns of behavior by interacting agents according to some local rules, but the exact patterns that emerge cannot be accurately predicted.

Far-from-equilibrium system: Such a system does not return to a regular state. It does not repeat itself, and it is nonlinear.

Human organization/system: It is a group comprising of two or more human beings as interacting agents, irrespective of the primary objective of the system.

Intelligence advantage: It is the advantage acquired by a human organization that structures/organizes around intrinsic and collective intelligence.

Intelligence strategy: It is the strategy stipulated in the intelligent organization theory that emphasizes the concept of organizing around intelligence, and the exploitation of attributes such as consciousness, awareness, mindfulness, intrinsic intelligence, collective intelligence, quality connectivity, organizational learning, corporate knowledge structure, mindful culture, and other intelligence-associated entities. It encompasses both a deliberate as well as an emergent component.

Intelligent organization/system: It is a human organization with a structure that engulfs an orgmind, an intelligence web, and an environment sensing and responding subsystem. Such an organization learns, adapts and evolves like an intelligent biological being.

Interdependency: A complex adaptive system is usually a sub-system of a larger complex adaptive system. Complex adaptive systems that affect/influence one another are interdependent.

Linearity: It is the proportionate relationship between cause and effect. Linear systems are modular and they can be examined using hierarchical decomposition.

Mindful culture: It is a form of supportive organizational culture that places equal emphasis/priority on internal and external focuses. The orgmindfulness aspect concentrates on the internal mental state of the interacting agents. The awareness aspect concentrates on the organization as an entity, and the changes in environmental factors (see mindfulness and orgmindfulness).

Mindfulness: It is a primary mental function that emerges from consciousness. It enables the human mind to keep track of its internal dynamic. Mindfulness ensures the emergence of better thoughts, words and actions in the mind. Thus, a mindful mind is highly aware of its internal state. (Mindfulness can be better achieved when the frequency of the brain wave is 13 Hz and below.)

Nonlinearity: It is the non-proportionate relationship between cause and effect. The output of a nonlinear system is not proportional to the input.

Orgmindfulness: It is a mental factor of an intelligent human organization that focuses on the mental state of the interacting agents continuously. It is responsible for elevating collective intelligence and nurturing a mindful culture.

Self-organization: It is the spontaneous process whereby the agents in a complex adaptive system interact without the guidance of a blueprint. It is also the principle underlying the emergence of forms manifest in physical, chemical, biological, ecological, social and cultural structures, that is, the spontaneous crystallization of order out of complex system. The dynamic is morphogenetic, that is, it favors certain states known as morphogenetic attractors. (Thus, there are certain advantages being a first mover.)

Strange attractor: It is one of the four states of dynamical systems with Feigenbaum number between 3 to below 3.7. It has some kind of patterned order and boundary, and when represented by a three dimensional phase diagram it appears like an infinite line that never goes through the same point twice but continues indefinitely within a bounded space.

Bibliography

Anderson, P. W., Arrow, K. J., and Pines, D. (1988). *The Economy as an Evolving Complex System*. New York: Addison-Wesley.

Arthur, B. (1994). *Increasing Returns and Path Dependence in the Economy*. Ann Arbor: University of Michigan.

Battram, A. (1996). *Navigating Complexity*. London: The Industrial Society.

Begun, J. W. (1994). Chaos and complexity: Frontiers of organization science. *Journal of Management Inquiry*, 3(4), 329–335.

Beijerse, R. P. (1999). Questions in knowledge management: Defining and conceptualizing a phenomenon. *Journal of Knowledge Management*, 3(2), 94–109.

Cleveland, H. (2002). *Nobody In Charge*. San Francisco: Josey-Bass.

De Geus. (1998). *The Living Company*. Cambridge: Harvard Business School Press.

Ehin, C. (2000). *Unleashing Intellectual Capital*. Boston: Butterworth-Heinnmann.

Einstein, A. (1954). *Ideas and Opinions*. New York: Crown Publishers.

Ellinor, J. and Gerald, G. (1998). *Dialogue: Rediscovering the Transforming Power of Conversation*. New York: John Wiley and Sons.

Gell-Mann, M. (1994). *The Quark and the Jaguar*. Boston: Little Brown.

Gladwin, T. N., Kennelly, J. J., and Krause, T. S. (1995). Shifting paradigms for sustainable development: Implications for management theory and research. *Academy of Management Review*, 20(4), 874–907.

Gleick, J. (1987). *Chaos: The Making of a New Science*. London: Heinemann.

Glynn, M. A. (1996). Innovative genius: A framework for relating individual and organizational intelligence to innovation. *Academy of Management Review*, 21(4).

Hayes, R. M. (1993). Measurement of information. *Information Processing and Management*, 29(1), 1–11.

Kauffman, S. A. (1989). The evolution of economic webs. In P.W.Anderson, K. J.Arrow and D. Pines (Eds.), *The Economy as an Evolving Complex System*, 125–146. New York: Addison-Wesley.

Kauffman, S. A. (1991). Antichaos and adaptation. *Scientific America*, 78–84.

Kauffman, S. A. (1993). *The Origins of Order: Self-Organization and Selection in Evolution*. Oxford: Oxford University Press.

Kelly, K. (1998). *New Rules for the New Economy*. New York: Viking.

Langloris, R. N. and Everett, M. J. (1992). Complexity, genuine uncertainty, and the economics of organization. *Human Systems Management*, 11, 67–75.

Langton, C. G. (1989). *Artificial Life*. New York: Addison-Wesley.

Levy, D. (1994). Chaos theory and strategy: Theory, application and management applications. *Strategic Management Journal*, 15, 167–178.

Lewin, R. (1992). *Complexity: Life at the Edge of Chaos*. New York: Macmillan.

Liang, T. Y. (1994). The basic entity model: A fundamental theoretical model of information and information processing. *Information Processing and Management*, 30(5), 647–661.

Liang, T. Y. (1996). The basic entity model: A theoretical model of information processing, decision making and information systems. *Information Processing and Management*, 32(4), 477–487.

Liang, T. Y. (1998). General information theory: Some macroscopic dynamics of the human thinking systems. *Information Processing and Management*, 34(2–3), 275–290.

Liang, T. Y. (2001). Nurturing intelligent human organizations: The nonlinear perspective of the human minds. *Human Systems Management*, 20(4), 281–289.

Liang T. Y. (2002). The inherent structure and dynamic of intelligent human organizations. *Human Systems Management*, 21(1), 9–19.

Liebowitz, J. (1999). *Building Organizational Intelligence*. New York: CRC Press.

McMaster, M. D. (1996). *The Intelligence Advantage: Organizing for Complexity*. Boston: Butterworth-Heinemann.

Merry, U. (1995). *Coping with Uncertainty*. Connecticut: Prager.

Nonaka, I., Toyama, R., and Konno, N. (2000). SECI, ba and leadership: A unified model of dynamic knowledge creation. *Long Range Planning*, 33, 5–34.

Overman, E. S. (1996). The new science of management: Chaos and quantum theory and method. *Journal of Public Administration Research and Theory*, 6(1), 75–89.

Pascale, R. T., Millemann, M., and Gioja, L. (2000). *Surfing the Edge of Chaos*. New York: Three Rivers Press.

Perry, T. S. (1995). Management chaos allows more creativity. *Research Technology Management*, 28(5), 14–17.

Pico, R. M. (2002). *Consciousness in Four Dimensions*. New York: McGraw-Hill.

Probst, G., Raub, S., and Romhardt, K. (2000). *Managing Knowledge*. West Sussex: John Wiley and Sons.

Senge, P., et al. (1994). *The Fifth Discipline: The Art and Practice of the Learning Organization*. London: Nicholas Brealey.

Shenhav, Y. (1995). From chaos to systems: The engineering foundations of organization theory, 1879–1932. *Administrative Science Quarterly*, 40, 557–585.

Simon, H. A. (1969/1988). *The Sciences of the Artificial*. Cambridge, MA: MIT Press.

Simon, H. A. (1972). Theories of bounded rationality. In C. B. McGuire and R. Radner (Eds.), *Decision and Organization: A Volume in Honour of Jacob Marschak*, 161–176. Amsterdam: North Holland Publishing Company.

Simon, H. A. (1976). *Administrative Behavior: A Study of Decision-Making Processes in Administrative Organizations*. New York: Macmillan.

Simon, H. A. (1989). Cognitive science: The process of human thinking. In *Public Lectures by Professor Herbert A. Simon* (Lee Kuan Yew Distinguished Visitor), National University of Singapore, 1–21.

Simon, H. A. (1989). Cognitive science: The nature of economic reality. In Public Lectures by Professor Herbert A. Simon (Lee Kuan Yew Distinguished Visitor), National University of Singapore, 22–43.

Stacey, R. D. (1991). *The Chaos Frontier*. Oxford: Butterworth-Heinemann.

Stacey, R. D. (1995). The science of complexity: An alternative perspective for strategic change processes. *Strategic Management Journal*, 16, 477–495.

Stacey, R. D. (1996). *Complexity in Creative Organizations*. San Francisco: Berrett-Kochler.

Stonier, T. (1990). *Information and the Internal Structure of the Universe: An Exploration into Information Physics*. London: Springer-Verlag.

Stonier, T. (1991). Towards a new theory of information. *Journal of Information Science*, 17(5), 257–263.

Stonier, T. (1992). *Beyond Information: The Natural History of Intelligence*. London: Springer-Verlag.

Sydanmaanlakka, P. (2002). *An Intelligent Organization*. Oxford: Capstone.

Thietart, R. A. and Forgues, B. (1995). Chaos theory and organization. *Organization Science*, 6(1), 19–31.

Waldrop, M. M. (1992). *Complexity: The Emerging Science at the Edge of Order and Chaos*. New York: Simon and Schuster.

Westley, F. and Vredenburg, H. (1997). Inter-organizational collaboration and the preservation of global biodiversity. *Organization Science*, 8(4), 381–403.

Winter, S. G. (2000). The satisficing principle in capacity learning. *Strategic Management Journal*, 21, 981–996.

Wolfram, S. (2002). *A New Kind of Science*. Canada: Wolfram Media, Inc.

Wood, R. (2000). *Managing Complexity*. London: Profile Books Ltd.

Zeleny, M. (1985). Spontaneous social orders. *General Systems*, 11(2), 117–131.

Zeleny, M. (1987). Autopoiesis. In *Systems and Control Encyclopedia*, 393–400. New York: Pergamon.

Zeleny, M. (1989). Knowledge as a new form capital. Part 1: Division and re-integration of knowledge. *Human Systems Management*, 8(1), 45–58.

Zeleny, M. (1989). Knowledge as a new form of capital. Part 2: Knowledge-based management systems. *Human Systems Management*, 8(2), 129–143.

Zeleny, M. (1990). Amoeba: The new generation of self-managing human systems. *Human Systems Management*, 9(2), 57–59.

Zeleny, M. (2003). *Human Systems Management*. Singapore: World Scientific.

Index